MY ANCESTOR WAS IN SERVICE

by Pamela Horn

D0982274

SOCIETY OF GENEALOGISTS ENTERPRISES LTD

Published by
Society of Genealogists Enterprises Limited
14 Charterhouse Buildings, Goswell Road, London EC1M 7BA
© The Society of Genealogists Enterprises and the authors 2009.

ISBN: 978-1-907199-01-1

British Library Cataloguing in Publication Data
A CIP Catalogue record for this book is available from the British Library.

The Society of Genealogists Enterprises Limited is a wholly owned
subsidiary of the Society of Genealogists, a registered charity, no 233701.

About the Author

Dr. Pamela Horn lectured in economic and social history at Oxford Polytechnic (now
Oxford Brookes University) for over twenty years. She has now retired but still gives
lectures to family history and local history groups. She has written a number of books
on social history topics covering the eighteenth to the twentieth centuries. They
include three on servant life during that period. These are *Flunkeys and Scullions. Life
below stairs in Georgian England* (2004), *The Rise and Fall of the Victorian Servant*
(latest edn. 2004) and *Life below Stairs in the Twentieth Century* (2003). Her most
recent books are *Life as a Victorian Lady* and *Life in a Victorian Household* (both
published 2007).

Cover Image - Photomontage composited from various sources within the Society of Genealogists'
'Special Collections' including Baker-Holl and Coatsworth. It also features a footman from a photo by
Arthur R. Inch ('Coachman and footmen of the Marquess of Londonderry, Londonderry House, Park
Lane; the wedding of HRH Princess Mary to Viscount Lascelles, 1922').

Graphic design and layout by Graham Collett.

ii

FOREWORD

In the late nineteenth century many families in Britain were involved in the world of Upstairs Downstairs. Either they had a family member who was in service or the household itself included at least one maid, so that by the end of the Victorian era approaching a third of all women in England and Wales had been a domestic worker at some time in their lives. Yet although the occupation employed so many people, it is difficult in the twenty-first century to discover just what their lives were like. This book seeks to give some guidance to researchers wishing to find out about relatives who were in service or who had themselves employed domestic staff.

It is significant that a government report in the mid-1940s on the *Post-War Organisation of Private Domestic Employment* should describe domestic work as 'the oldest, the largest and the most unorganised form of women's employment ... A thoughtless mistress with a touch of the tyrant in her composition can make life a perpetual fret for her staff. Or by tact and consideration she may make its burden almost inappreciable ... Alternative employment on a large scale was not available and a host of women consequently had to submit to conditions sometimes very onerous but which varied enormously from household to household.'[1] It is this situation that has to be explored.

I should like to express my thanks to the National Trust for permission to quote from the Disraeli papers deposited in the Bodleian Library, Oxford. I am also grateful to the staff at the many libraries and record offices where I have worked for much efficient assistance. Their help has made this book possible.

Pamela Horn

CONTENTS

FIGURES

1. The reputed indifference of servants to their employer's demand for attention is illustrated in this cartoon from the Mayhew brothers' novel, *The Greatest Plague of Life* (1847). It had the caption: 'Oh, ah! Let 'em ring again!'

2. Status and servant ceremonial. The elaborate livery of the coachman and footmen employed by the Marquess of Londonderry with his state coach outside Londonderry House, Park Lane on the occasion of the wedding of HRH Princess Mary to Viscount Lascelles in 1922. (Arthur R. Inch)

3. The notorious weakness of butlers for sampling the contents of their employer's cellar is highlighted in this *Punch* cartoon (1873).

4. Nannies at a children's birthday party c.1903. Note the elaborate dress of the nurse on the right, indicating her 'superior' status. (Mr. V.C. Buckley).

5. A naive young maid-of-all-work questioned by her employer as to why his breakfast had been delayed. (*Punch*, 1852).

6. Mrs. G. Simpson, cook in an upper-middle-class household with her scullery maid, 1936. (Mrs. J. Simpson).

7. The idleness and arrogance of footmen and the anxiety of the lady's maid concerning her duties are depicted in this *Punch* cartoon of 1875.

8. Nurse Abberley with three members of the Irving family in Wales c.1904. A nanny was an important and formative influence in the lives of her young charges. (Mr. E. J. B. Irving).

9. John Henry Inch when employed as a butler at Marlands, Itchingfield, Horsham with his two footmen, c.1922. (Arthur R. Inch).

10. Estate staff at Thame Park, Oxfordshire, home of the Wykeham-Musgrave family c.1900. The group includes gardeners, grooms, bricklayers and other outdoor servants. (Centre for Oxfordshire Studies and Oxfordshire County Council Photographic Archive).

11. Advertisement for outdoor workers in *The Shooting Times and British Sportsman*, 12 October, 1895. Several of the advertisements inserted by gamekeepers mentioned their height and weight.

12. A gardener and gardener's boy with a potato planter c.1900. (Centre for Oxfordshire Studies and Oxfordshire County Council Photographic Archive).

13. An advertisement in *The Shooting Times and British Sportsman*, 12 January, 1895 suggesting to gamekeepers one way of tackling poaching problems.

14. Advertising for servants was one way of recruiting new staff. These advertisements appeared in the *Buckinghamshire Advertiser and Aylesbury News*, 15 August, 1891.

15. Girls at a domestic servants' training school conducted at Headington Hill Hall, Oxford, 1913. The school was financed by charity. (Centre for Oxfordshire Studies and Oxfordshire County Council Photographic Archive).

16. Trainees learning new cooking skills at the Oxford Centre of the National Institute of Houseworkers, June 1949. (TUC Library).

17. Maid being questioned by her mistress about a meeting with her 'young man' outside the garden gate. The usual rule was 'no followers allowed'. (*Punch*, 1871)

18. Maids enjoying a tea party in the garden of Garsington Rectory, Oxfordshire, in the 1890s. They appear rather self-conscious in what must have been, for them, an unfamiliar situation. (Centre for Oxfordshire Studies and Oxfordshire County Council Photographic Archive).

19. The servant as criminal. Ada Mary Wood, aged 16, was imprisoned in Aylesbury gaol for two months with hard labour for stealing a gold locket from her mistress in 1871. (Centre for Buckinghamshire Studies).

CHAPTER ONE
Servant Keeping

Introduction

'**M**y goodness,' declared Jane Welsh Carlyle to a friend, 'why make bits of apologies for writing about the servants - as if "the servants" were not a most important - a most fearful item in our female existence!' Jane was married to the eminent Victorian literary figure, Thomas Carlyle, and her comment reflected the concern of many wives and daughters about the recruitment and retention of domestic staff. It came at a time when servant keeping was considered not merely an aid in running often inconvenient and cluttered homes with few labour-saving appliances, but as a symbol of social standing. In addition many families were large and as wives spent much of their reproductive life pregnant or recovering from the birth of a baby, help was needed in caring for the children. In 1880 *The Servants' Practical Guide*, one of a growing number of manuals on household management, firmly stated that: 'Without the constant co-operation of well-trained servants, domestic machinery is completely thrown out of gear, and the best bred of hostesses placed at a disadvantage.'

Significantly, when Seebohm Rowntree conducted his famous survey of the people of York in 1899, he made the keeping or not keeping of domestic

servants the dividing line between 'the working classes and those of a higher social scale'. For this reason, countless families strove to recruit a maid even if, at its lowest level, this meant hiring a daily charwoman or a teenage 'skivvy' from the local workhouse, to whom they paid a wage of one shilling (5p) or so a week. Workhouse girls were usually too small and clumsy to be employed in fashionable homes, where a good appearance was considered necessary to impress family and friends. At Alderley Edge, Cheshire, Katharine Hopkinson, daughter of a successful Manchester businessman, recalled that in that socially competitive environment, a mistress's status could be affected by such matters as the way in which the parlourmaid opened the front door to visitors: 'the trimmer the maid and the more distant her manner the more intimidating the formality of one's entrance.'

Despite the large number of servants employed, with 1.29 million at work in England and Wales in 1881 and 1.3 million two decades later, according to the official census reports, the occupation remains largely hidden, with details of individual lives and careers difficult to unearth. General information on the daily round of many of them can be found in household management manuals and in journals, as well as in the letters, diaries and memoirs of their employers. In a few cases the reminiscences and autobiographies of former domestics also survive. These have been published in a few cases, but others can be found in county record offices and libraries in manuscript or taped form. Information on what employers expected of their servants may be gleaned from advertisements of staff vacancies in the press, as in *The Gardeners' Chronicle* of 7 January, 1882, when a Bournemouth employer seeking a head gardener specified that the successful candidate should be without children and a member of the Church of England, while his wife was to act as 'a Laundry Woman'.

In the case of those employed in stately homes, wages books, servants' record books, and correspondence may identify particular employees and give details of their careers. Where workers were recruited from charities like the Foundling Hospital in London, or from poor law institutions, the records of these will give information on the youngsters sent to service or being trained for a domestic career. But for the vast bulk of domestics, employed in small households and growing up within their own families, this information is rarely available.

Throughout it is important to remember that most servants employed within the home were female, since women were cheaper to employ, easier to discipline, and more readily recruited than the menfolk, since they had fewer alternative employment outlets. Only the wealthiest families could afford a butler or footman, or even a page, although it was recognised that a retinue of male retainers was a sign of a family's wealth and importance. Loelia, Duchess of Westminster, recalled that

Figure 1. The Greatest Plague of Life (1847): 'Oh, ah! Let 'em ring again!'

although her parents moved in exclusive social circles they were regarded as 'dreadfully badly off' because they could only afford five maids, a manservant, a boy and two gardeners. Their friends were 'mostly people who had too many servants to count'. The 'luxury' aspect of male servant recruitment was indicated by the fact that from the 1770s to 1937 a tax was imposed on their employment, and some of these servant licences still survive. The Society of Genealogists holds a manuscript index to the employers listed in these records for the year 1780. Between 1869 and 1937 the tax amounted to a modest 15s. (75p) per servant per annum.

In 1851, when there were just over 751,000 females in private indoor service, they outnumbered their male colleagues by around ten to one. By 1881, when their total had reached over 1.2 million, they exceeded the males by twenty-two to one, and that trend continued to the end of the century and beyond as regards indoor staff. Not far short of half of the women were under the age of twenty, and of girls aged between fifteen and twenty years of age it was estimated in 1881 that one in three was a domestic servant.

In these circumstances it is not surprising that the *General Report of the 1881 Population Census for England and Wales* should note that indoor servants were the most numerous group of workers in the country, exceeding the next group, the agricultural labourers, by some fifty per cent.[1]

However, the proportion of servants within the population varied widely from one area to another. London was the major draw, with about one in five of the nation's maids working in the capital in 1881 and about one in six in 1911. Also important were what the 1881 Census Report called the towns of 'habitual resort of the wealthier classes', such as Bath and Brighton. In Bath in that year about one in nine of the total population was a servant, while in Brighton it was one in eleven. But in urban areas in the industrial north and the Midlands girls often preferred the greater freedom of factory life to the close personal supervision and the limitations on leisure pursuits and dress that went with domestic service. To be a servant in industrial Lancashire was regarded by many working people as something to be ashamed of and as socially inferior to other kinds of occupation. Many of the county's maids were drawn from agricultural districts in Yorkshire, Cumberland, Wales and Ireland, where alternative female jobs were difficult to find. Like Winifred Foley, who grew up in a village in the Forest of Dean, they discovered that when they reached the age of fourteen - and sometimes before that - they were expected to get their feet 'under someone else's table'. 'The bony finger of poverty was pushing me out into an alien world', wrote Winifred, 'away from the little corner I knew and the family I loved'.[2] Soon after this she obtained her first place in London.

In Lancashire in 1881 it was estimated that just one in thirty of the total population was a maid, and in County Durham, with its expanding coal industry, that ratio was one in thirty-one. This meant that in modest households in industrial towns a daughter or other relative often took on the duties of a maid and might be so designated in the census returns.

Who Were the Servant Keepers?

It was during the 1850s and 1860s that the number of domestics grew particularly rapidly, at a time when there was an expansion in professional and manufacturing activity in the country and a consequent rise in the total of families able to afford to keep a maid. The General Report of the 1871 Census of Population recorded sourly that, 'Wives and daughters at home do now less domestic work than their predecessors: hence the excessive demand for female servants and the consequent rise in wages.' Later in the century this increasing affluence affected the recruitment of outdoor servants, too, with the numbers of grooms and particularly gardeners growing rapidly in the 1890s.

At the summit of the servant-keeping hierarchy were the richest aristocrats with their numerous retainers and estates constituting a 'settlement as large as a small village'. At Welbeck Abbey in Nottinghamshire in the early twentieth century, the Duke of Portland had a staff of around 320, including fourteen housemaids and thirty-eight male and female servants in the kitchen and allied departments. Overall control and supervision of them was exercised by the senior members of staff. As one of the footmen, Frederick John Gorst, recalled: 'The estate of Welbeck Abbey was more like a principality than anything else; there were scores of people working beside me whom I did not know... Within the borders of Welbeck Abbey, His Grace the Duke of Portland wielded an almost feudal indisputable power'.

Those working in such households often enjoyed some of the reflected glory of their employer's high status. Albert Thomas, who became third footman to a well-known sporting duke, thought this was 'a lovely job ... to be sure, hard work and plenty of it, but ... elevating work, ... we were respected by the townsfolk'. Membership of such households could also help to secure further promotion for those anxious to make a career in service. When A. Hood, a cook-housekeeper employed at Dalby Hall in Leicestershire, applied in 1912 for a similar position in the household of the Earl of Rosebery, she was careful to point out that she understood 'French Cookery' and had been 'accustomed to large dinner parties ... There are 14 servants kept here'.[3]

But some domestics were more cynical about master-servant relations. Eric Horne, who boasted that he had spent fifty-seven years in service 'with the Nobility and Gentry', remarked on the 'vast abyss between gentry and servants ... Servants are looked upon as a part of the furniture of the house; live furniture, nothing more. If the live furniture is in the town house and is wanted in the country house, or vice versa, it is simply moved there. If a piece of the live furniture gets broken in body or health, the gentry simply say: - "Chuck it out and get another. It's all the same to us".' [4]

The majority of servants did not work in large households, however. In fact the biggest single category of female domestics was the maid-of-all-work, who was probably employed on her own or, at most, alongside one or two fellow members of staff. In 1851, three-quarters of all female servants fell into this 'general' category and even in 1871, which was the last year the Census Report, differentiated on a national basis between categories, they comprised nearly two-thirds of the total. Yet, at a time when employers were beginning to seek more specialised staff, it is significant that the number of housemaids, cooks and nursemaids recorded increased far more rapidly over the period.

Those who fell within the servant-keeping classes thus varied widely in social position and income. In rural market towns like Wantage, then in Berkshire, Thame in Oxfordshire, and Fakenham in Norfolk in 1871, where around one household in six kept a resident maid, about two-fifths of the employers were small tradesmen, such as drapers, grocers, plumbers, coal merchants, corn dealers and the like. Some had very limited means, as Mrs. Lizzie Gale discovered at Wylam in Northumberland in the early 1920s. She was hired by a corn merchant's family and remembered how they had 'just brought themselves up from nothing ...[T]here, *it* was a bad-meat place. You just got one tatie each ... and a tomato was cut up between me and the mistress ...And everything was under lock and key, even to your black lead that you did your fireplace with'.[5]

In country districts girls worked on farms and were often expected to help on the land at the busy seasons, as well as assist in the dairy. Florence Stowe went to a farmhouse on the Warwickshire/Oxfordshire border early in the twentieth century when she was fourteen. She recalled that her pre-breakfast tasks included blackleading the kitchen range, lighting the fire, cleaning the dining room, stairs and hall, and then heating the milk for the cowman to feed to the calves. After breakfast the washing up included scalding the dairy utensils. If the hay harvest were delayed by bad weather, she had to help in the fields, too. One afternoon each week was devoted to making the butter, 'a 2-hour work and about 30 to 40 lb. to

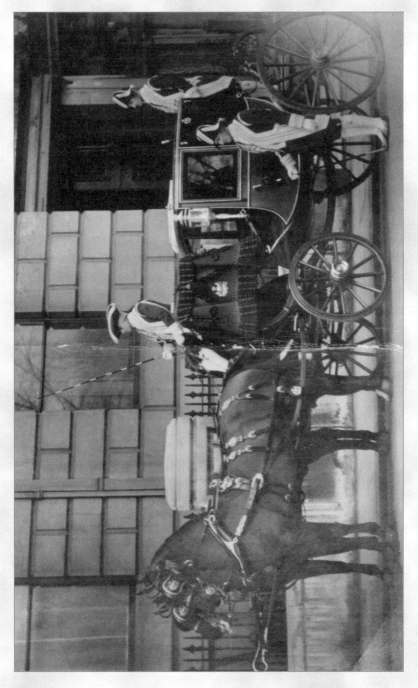

Figure 2. Coachman and footmen of the Marquess of Londonderry, Londonderry House, Park Lane; the wedding of HRH Princess Mary to Viscount Lascelles, 1922 (Arthur R. Inch).

pot up, weigh, mark, ready for market'. She also brought in the wood and coal needed for the fires and lent a hand with the washing and ironing.[6]

Higher up the servant-keeping scale were the professional classes, such as doctors, clergymen, lawyers and bank managers, as well as the more substantial businessmen. They probably aimed to recruit about three servants, since that was considered the minimum necessary if a household were to be 'complete in all its functions'. In the late Victorian period these normally comprised a cook, housemaid and parlourmaid, or if there were young children in the family, a nursemaid. According to Charles Booth, who conducted a social survey of the people of London in the 1890s, the 'most comfortable & desirable households' for maids were 'middle class families keeping three servants, they receive more individual attention from the mistress & their physical wants are well attended to'.[7] They were, perhaps, following Mrs. Isabella Beeton's advice in her famous *Book of Household Management* (1861) when she declared that as 'with the commander of an army, or the leader of any enterprise, so is it with the mistress of a house. Her spirit will be seen through the whole establishment; and just in proportion as she performs her duties intelligently and thoroughly, so will her domestics follow in her path.' The Booth collection at LSE Archives contains the original records from Booth's survey into life and labour in London, dating from 1886 to 1903. (The Charles Booth Online Archive is a searchable resource giving access to archive material within the archive collections of the Archives Division of the Library of the London School of Economics and Political Science and the Senate House Library http://booth.lse.ac.uk/)

Mrs. Beeton took to task those women who criticised their servants to their friends, reminding them that there were 'few families of respectability, from the shopkeeper in the next street to the nobleman whose mansion dignifies the next square, which do not contain among their dependents attached and useful servants; ... The sensible master and the kind mistress know, that if servants depend on them for their means of living, in their turn they are dependent on their servants for very many of the comforts of life'.

Servant keepers did not always follow these strictures. Some tested their servants' honesty and diligence by concealing coins under the edges of carpets and mats, to see whether they were found and, if so, were handed over. Others changed their servants' names to fit in with an established custom. Sarah Jane Reeves, who grew up at Manor Farm, Catmore, in Berkshire during the 1850s and 1860s, recalled that her mother kept two maids. One was middle-aged and helped with the cooking and

"ON THE FACE OF IT."

Host. "I DON'T LIKE THIS LAFITTE HALF SO WELL AS THE LAST, BINNS. HAVE YOU NOTICED ANY DIFFERENCE?"

New Butler. "WELL, SIR, FOR MYSELF I DON'T DRINK CLARET; I FIND PORT AGREES WITH ME SO MUCH BETTER!!"

Figure 3. The weakness of butlers for sampling the contents of their employer's cellar. Punch cartoon (1873).

the dairy. The other, a young girl from the village, was expected to stay for about two years only while she received basic training in domestic work. 'Their names were always changed to Ann and Mary when in our service'. A few mistresses also laid down racial or religious restrictions, so that Lady Astor at Cliveden would not recruit Roman Catholics even in the twentieth century. Some, like the novelist, Virginia Woolf and her artist sister, Vanessa Bell, seem to have had an ambivalent attitude towards their servants. That applied even to those who were with them many years. Whilst recognising that they could not manage without domestic help, given the needs of their social life, they nonetheless appear to have resented this dependency. In 1910, even before she was married, Virginia complained of the inconvenience of having maids living at close quarters in a small house. She felt her two domestics 'made everything pompous, and heavy-footed'. 'Why we have them, I can't think', she told Vanessa. Later she conceded, 'If you have a house you must have servants.'

Even in modest homes there were clear social distinctions drawn by mistresses in respect of their servants. In one case, for example, at the end of the 1930s, a teenage general maid employed at Welford in Northamptonshire was not allowed to use the front door or the front stairs when going about her duties. As was customary, she ate her meals alone in the kitchen and on warm days in the summer, during her free time in the afternoon, 'when it was very hot in the kitchen, she was expected to keep out of sight of the garden and sit behind the door in the kitchen or in the back scullery.' [8] As far as possible when they were at work maids were expected to render themselves invisible, and to take no part in their employers' conversations unless invited to do so. Only with the children of the family might a more relaxed atmosphere prevail.

Some ambitious families, anxious to have the benefit of several servants but lacking the means to pay for them, arranged for their solitary maid to fulfil a variety of functions. Winifred Foley in her mid-teens went to work for a middle-class family with two children in Cheltenham. Their limited resources meant that her weekly wage was just 5 shillings. There were petty distinctions made as regards her food, too, and that was not uncommon in many households. 'My mistress bought my bacon separate from theirs; it was narrow streaky rashers cut very thin, and one of these was put out each morning for my breakfast.' To obtain her allotted slices of bread she had to go into the dining-room to ask for them and they were then handed over by the employer. But most of all Winifred recalled the multiplicity of domestic tasks she was expected to carry out:

'They were in need of a strong young fool - one who could be house-maid from six till one for cleaning the house, then parlour-maid for waiting at table, then nanny for the children's afternoon outings, then washerwoman in the evenings. They needed a creature that would run on very little fuel and would not question her lot ... I became quite a nimble worker, especially as, on the spartan diet she provided, I had no surplus flesh to hold me back.' [9]

She remained in this household for six months, that 'being the limit of my endurance ... I escaped to home as soon as I reasonably could, and determined never again to look for a job where my employers were trying to keep up an appearance beyond their means'.

Winifred was not alone in moving rapidly from place to place. To the annoyance of many servant keepers, girls often remained for only a few months before looking round for a fresh post. Perhaps they were seeking higher pay, or a more congenial mistress, or wider experience, or merely looking for a change. A survey conducted in the 1890s suggested that over half of the sample investigated in England and Wales had stayed in the same situation for under two years; more than a third had been there for less than twelve months.[10]

There was, of course, a loyal minority who stayed with the same family for many years. They might end by being remembered in their employer's Will or, especially in large households, living in the household as a pensioner. This was true of the long-serving housekeeper of the Earl and Countess of Carnarvon, Mrs. Gaymour, in the mid-nineteenth century. Another long-serving maid was Grace Wiggens (née Germany) who stayed with Vanessa Bell and her partner, Duncan Grant, for fifty years. In later years, after Grace's marriage, her husband acted as the family gardener.

The Dukes of Bedford were noted as paying generous pensions to many Woburn servants when they retired. The ninth Duke, who succeeded to the title in 1872, paid out about £1,000 in pensions to thirty-two old servants. Three were senior staff, rewarded for their long service with £50 a year each. They included John Sprague, the house steward, who received his when he was seventy-five. He had already been granted an annuity under the Will of the seventh Duke, who had died in 1861. Mary Brittain, who had served the family for forty-nine years, first as needlewoman and then as housekeeper at Endsleigh, another of the Bedford properties, was given her pension at the age of sixty-five. Many of the others on the ninth Duke's list of pensioners were outdoor servants, such as John Bowles, who was the ducal coachman for twenty-one years. According to Adeline Hartcup, the longest career seems to have been that of James Keens, 'who began by working in the kitchen gardens, went on to do everyday jobs in the park and woods, and finally chalked up a total of sixty years outside service.[11]

A study of the collection of the abstracts of wills collected by the Bank of England 1717-1845 and held at the Society of Genealogists shows a surprising number of former female servants who themselves left wills having been given Bank stock and annuities as pensions. The abstracts can be found at the Society of Genealogists and are indexed online at www.britishorigins.com

But perhaps the last word on this matter of long service can be left to Mildred White, a Cheltenham cook-housekeeper, who had been with her then mistress for sixteen years. 'We both know that I could get three times the wage she is able to pay', she wrote in the spring of 1945, 'but I have not met anyone else that I would work for in this capacity. I see so many who are so selfish, who treat their maids as machines, give them little or no comforts, and certainly no respect ... We have always shown the greatest respect for each other ... I am so *very*, *very* happy in my work.'[12]

Figure 4. Nannies at a children's birthday party c1903 (Mr. V.C. Buckley).

CHAPTER TWO
The Daily Round: Indoor Servants

General Background

The growing number of books on household management published in the nineteenth century bear witness to what Margaret Willes has called 'the complex and ingenious cleaning skills required' in looking after homes at a time when there were few mechanical aids available to lighten the domestic load. The manuals also instructed workers, particularly those going to their first place, on the attitude they should adopt towards their master and mistress. Typically, Samuel and Sarah Adams in *The Complete Servant* (1825) advised 'young persons, on ... first entering into service ...[to] devote themselves to the control of those whom they engage to serve ... The grand foundation of your good character must be industry, fidelity to your employers, and an inviolable attachment to truth, both in words and deeds'.

Nonetheless the tasks performed by individual workers depended not merely on their personal relationship with their employer but on the size and wealth of the household and its composition. They depended on a servant's gender, too, with males more likely to be called on to play a ceremonial role and the women a functional one.

15

Men were more costly to employ and could also present discipline problems. For this reason *The Servants' Practical Guide* recommended widows and single women to recruit parlourmaids rather than footmen, adding darkly that 'a man-servant is proverbially inclined to take advantage of his position when there is no master to keep him in check.' J. H. Walsh, in his *Manual of Domestic Economy* (1874 edition) took a similar view, considering a man-servant 'an expensive luxury'. However, he admitted that those who went 'much into society, either in London or the country [were] almost compelled to inflict this nuisance on themselves, as it is considered by many people one of the tests of their position, and if it is not carried out, they will find themselves excluded from the visiting lists of people with whom they may desire to associate on equal terms.[1]

Charles Booth, too, drew attention to the link between a footman's appearance and the wages he could command. A first footman who was 5 ft. 10 in. or 6 ft. could expect £32 to £40 a year, whereas one who was only 5 ft. 6 in. would be unlikely to receive more than £30 a year. For this reason advertisements in the press for footmen often specified that the successful candidate must be tall. One such appeared in the *Oxford Times* of 21 March, 1891, when a Mrs. Blandy Jenkins living near Abingdon was seeking a footman to work under a butler. He was to be 'not over 18 years of age, ... tall and of good appearance'. Applicants were to state their height and the wage they required, but there was a proviso that 'No London servants need apply'. Presumably this was because they were either thought to be too sophisticated for the countryside and would exert a bad influence on the rest of the staff, or were considered likely to become disillusioned with the slow pace of provincial life and depart speedily.

Not all servants worked in private houses. Some were employed in hotels, schools, hospitals, clubs and other institutions, where a more commercial spirit might prevail. Those engaged in lodging houses were considered to have the hardest positions, being at the beck and call of the boarders as well as the landlady, and usually poorly paid.

As industrialisation and commercial practices exerted a growing influence in the economy at large, there was a change in the management of servants, too. This manifested itself during the nineteenth century in a move away from a task-oriented approach to their deployment to one concerned with punctuality and adherence to a specific programme of jobs to be performed. Contracts were drawn up stating the duties - and the limitations - placed on staff, including senior domestics. This could apply, for instance, to the giving of orders to tradesmen, which might afford the

BACHELOR HOUSEKEEPING.

Mr. Brown. "PRAY, JANE, WHAT ON EARTH IS THE REASON I AM KEPT WAITING FOR MY BREAKFAST IN THIS WAY?"

Jane. "PLEASE, SIR, THE ROLLS ISN'T COME, AND THERE'S NO BREAD IN THE HOUSE!"

Mr. Brown. "NOW, UPON MY WORD! HOW CAN YOU ANNOY ME WITH SUCH TRIFLES? NO *BREAD*, THEN BRING ME SOME *TOAST*." *(Exit Jane in dismay.*

Figure 5. A naive young maid questioned by her employer (Punch, 1852).

unscrupulous opportunities for fraud. At Englefield House in Berkshire in the mid-Victorian years, the butler was firmly informed that his master, Mr. Benyon, kept the keys to the wine cellar and gave out wine as it was wanted, 'of which you keep an account. I order every thing and pay for every thing - you order nothing except by my direction ... You give out the Ale yourself [to the servants] in a fixed allowance.' As with other members of staff in this household, the butler was also told that his master would not pay medical bills should he become ill, and he and the rest of the servants were to attend morning prayers.[2]

In many households detailed timetables were provided as well, laying down precisely when tasks were to be performed. Lavinia Swainbank remembered her dismay when she received her first timetable as an under-housemaid. It began at 6.30 am, when she rose, and, as she noted ruefully, it seemed designed to turn 'an ordinary human being into something resembling a well-oiled machine'. However, she learned to cope.[3]

A flavour of what was expected is provided by the timetable for a house-parlourmaid drawn up around 1910 by Marion Sambourne, the widow of a leading cartoonist on the satirical magazine *Punch*. Marion was then living in Kensington with her unmarried son, Roy, and there were usually three or four maids, with a groom recruited from time to time. The house-parlourmaid was in charge of the morning room, the dining room and the pantry, as well as assisting once a week in a thorough cleaning of the drawing-room. She was to be downstairs by 7 am. and was to begin her day by dusting, sweeping and shaking the rugs. Next she had to clean the brasses in the dining room, as well as wipe over the inside of the windows and lay the breakfast table:

8 am	Breakfast kitchen.
8.30 am	Sweep, dust and polish morning room. Water plants - keep brass and silver well polished. All plants and vases watered, dead flowers and leaves removed. Take up my breakfast.
9 am	Mr. Roy's breakfast. Put out Mr. Roy's hat, gloves, stick or umbrella. Have Mr. R's books ready.
9.30 am	Fetch my tray and put away Mr. Roy's clothes and take to brush. See to Mr. R's silver and his drawers tidy.
10 am	Take away and wash up breakfast things & see to drawing room silver.
11 am	Prepare two rooms for special cleaning, after which lay luncheon.
1.15 pm	Dress for luncheon.
1.30 pm	Lunch. Look through Mr. Roy's clothes and keep all mended.
4.30 pm	Tea.

6.30 pm	Put out Mr. Roy's evening clothes. To have dinner table ready laid by 7 pm
8 pm	Dinner.

Special days cleaning

Monday	Dining room floor polished, brasses, window sills washed. New paper in cupboards if necessary.
Tuesday	All silver in dining room, drawing-room. Help with flowers.
Wednesday	Pantry - scrub and clean thoroughly.
Thursday	Morning room.
Friday	Special silver day, all drawing-room silver as well.
Saturday	Drawing-room. Entire charge of Mr. Roy's clothes, to pack and unpack them when he leaves and returns from visits, and wait and attend to all gentlemen visitors.

As Mrs. Sambourne was a widow the parlourmaid was only responsible for her son's clothes, while the housemaid took on some of the duties of a lady's maid.[4]

As Leonore Davidoff points out, servants in these households had an important subsidiary role in shielding family members from the demands of the outside world. It was the kitchen staff who dealt with tradesmen and other commercial callers at the back door, while the butler, footman or parlourmaid coped with 'the ritual of calls and card-leaving by social equals at the front door'. That included informing visitors whether the mistress was 'at home' to receive them.[5]

Within the household, bells were rung for attention and a servant was expected to respond to them speedily. A lady's maid at Great Glen manor in Leicestershire remembered how even in the 1930s they were frequently being rung. The row of bells was located in the basement 'and if we were up on the top, ... one of us would come running down three flights of stairs and then have to go back up and knock' on the door of whoever had rung. 'You used to have to come running from the other end of the house'.

Most domestics, however worked in smaller one or two-servant establishments, and in these mistresses might work alongside them, carrying out some of the chores themselves. Jane Welsh Carlyle taught her young maids how to prepare the beef broth, broiled chops and baked milk puddings her husband favoured, as well as doing some of the cleaning, including blacking the parlour grate and making her own bed when the maid proved particularly young and incompetent. [6] Mrs. Beeton noted that many servants began their career in the household of a small tradesman's wife, who might prove to be what she called a 'very rough specimen of the feminine gender'. Sometimes the girls were subjected to bullying and even physical abuse, as court records and newspaper accounts confirm. The short-lived *Domestic Servants' Advertiser* of 20 May, 1913 reported one such case at Evesham Police Court, when a mistress was charged with ill treating her fourteen-year-old maid, Rose Rutter. The girl claimed she was beaten almost daily by the mistress and had her head banged against the wall. She was also kicked, and there were bruises all over her body. The mistress denied the charge, stating that the girl was clumsy and had sustained the bruises by falling downstairs and running into the door-post. Her story was not believed and she was fined £10, including costs, or in default two months' imprisonment. Occasionally the mistreatment was so severe that it led to the maid's death.[7] The fact that the girls were living away from home meant there were few people to whom they could turn for help when they experienced abuse.

For the minority of workers employed in large households, a strict hierarchy existed, with tasks minutely subdivided in a way that gave few opportunities for demarcation disputes. Lady Astor wrote of there being 'a sort of aristocracy amongst servants in those days'. They were 'specialists in their own job. The etiquette of the servants' hall was far stricter and more involved than in other parts of the house, the social distinctions more rigid'.[8] The house steward or the butler headed the male servants, and the housekeeper, or in smaller establishments, the cook-housekeeper, controlled the females, while the chef or cook supervised those working in the kitchen. The lady's maid and the valet occupied a special position because of their close relationship to the employer. Only in the second half of the twentieth century did this situation change markedly, as servant shortage and economic pressures led to posts being merged, so that the butler might also act as a chauffeur, and his wife as cook-housekeeper and supervisor of charwomen.

In the case of landed families with several properties, some members of staff would move around with their master and mistress as they migrated between residences or settled in their London town house for the Season. At Longleat, the Marchioness of Bath recalled there was an indoor staff of forty-three at the beginning of the twentieth century with seventeen of them accompanying the family when they moved to the capital for the Season, from late April or May to the end of July. Usually some of the housemaids and probably the housekeeper would remain behind at the country seat to carry out spring cleaning while the family was away, and there would be a London housekeeper to take charge of the town house. After the spring cleaning had been completed the most vulnerable furniture would be swathed in protective covers until the employers returned. At such times the servants would be on board wages, whereby they were paid a specific daily or weekly sum and were expected to cater for themselves out of this. If they were frugal that offered a chance to amass some savings.

Figure 6. Mrs. G. Simpson, cook in an upper-middle-class household with her scullery maid, 1936. (Mrs. J. Simpson).

While the spring cleaning was in progress, extra staff might be brought in on a temporary basis, including the wives of outdoor workers on the estate. In some households, however, part-time helpers formed a regular part of the staff, so that at Longleat a daily woman worked in the kitchen, presumably carrying out the heavier scrubbing and cleaning.

In large establishments the senior servants occupied the position of surrogate employers, directing their juniors and reproving them when they failed to carry out their work satisfactorily. Many of the seniors were strict taskmasters, as their employers expected them to be. This was partly because of the need to maintain a high standard of service, but also because staff were often young and high-spirited. At Englefield House, for example, in 1891 only six of the nineteen indoor servants were aged thirty or over, and that was fairly typical. Eric Horne, who eventually became a butler himself, admitted that it was in the power of upper servants 'to make the younger ones lives livable, (sic) or a perfect hell'. [9] The juniors rarely saw their master or mistress, since they were expected to be 'invisible' when going about their duties, using separate staircases and keeping out of the way when the family was about. Agnes Graham, who worked in a large Liverpool household around the beginning of the 1930s, remembered the servants living 'behind a green baize door.' She only saw her mistress when she was appointed and when she gave in her notice, an event which the mistress greeted with evident disgust.[10]

The senior staff had their own servants, too, so that the stillroom maids worked for the housekeeper and the hall-boy or usher for the butler. Ernest King observed drily that as a hall-boy he was introduced to the realities of servant life by 'being a servant to the servants; the table in the servants' hall to lay, the staff cutlery to clean and the staff meals to put on the table. In the butler's pantry I spent most of my time at the washing-up tub. My hands and arms in winter were chapped up to the elbow. My day's work also included cleaning all windows in the house, all knives and all boots, the family's, the butler's and any visitors'. Similarly, George Washington, who was a steward's room boy at Holland House in London during the 1930s, remembered that his special duties were to look after the steward's room, where the senior servants had their meals, and to valet the butler. That meant rising at 5.30 am to wake the butler at 6 am with a mug of tea and a can of hot water for washing. 'I would look out his clothes and clean his boots'. He then began lighting some of the fires and because the 'odd man' employed to do miscellaneous chores was too old to perform the more laborious of them young George had to step in, carrying heavy buckets of coal around the house. He also scrubbed the long passage in the servants' quarters and drew the ale which was provided for the servants to drink. But there were perquisites in that he inherited

HOW THE LUGGAGE IS LOST.

Lady's-Maid. "THOMAS, WHY DON'T YOU SEE THE BOXES PUT IN THE VAN? THEY MAY BE LOST!"
Thomas. "I'M NOT GOING TO TROUBLE MYSELF WITH ALL THAT THERE LUGGAGE. IT'S THE PORTER'S BUSINESS. HE'S PAID FOR IT!"

Figure 7. The idleness and arrogance of footmen and the anxiety of the lady's maid concerning her duties are depicted in this Punch cartoon of 1875.

the empty wine bottles and corks that came down from the dining-room when Lord Ilchester was in residence. These he sold at a small profit.[11]

Within most larger households tensions arose between members of staff and there were quarrels because they had to spend so much time in one another's company, with few opportunities to mix with outsiders. At Badminton House, home of the Duke of Beaufort, the young footman, Charles Dean, remembered the bitter enmity between the butler and the chauffeurs in a house that had been traditionally dominated by an interest in horses: 'the motor car was seen as a menace to our way of life so chauffeurs were treated as lepers'.[12] Rapid staff changes, too, usually indicated that there were problems. At Cliveden the newly-married Astors had five butlers between October 1906 and July 1909. Two were dismissed within months for drunkenness, one left after three months, being described as 'honest but bad manager' and a fourth was condemned as 'capable but too big an idea of his position'. Likewise at Nuneham Park in Oxfordshire, where there had been just two butlers or house stewards in a fifteen-year period from June 1862 to November 1877, during the next five and a half years there were six holders of those positions. The wages books merely give their names and the amount of their pay but not the reasons for their rapid departures.[13] However, as Eric Horne drily commented, in other occupations 'one has to be with objectionable people only during working hours. In service one has to be with them always, have meals with them, living always in the same house, night and day'.

Meals were eaten separately in these households, with the senior staff the steward, the butler, the housekeeper, the lady's maid. the valet and perhaps the head nurse - taking their meals in the steward's or housekeeper's room (labelled the 'pug's parlour' by irreverent juniors). They only joined the rest of the staff in the servants' hall for the meat course of the mid-day dinner. For this they solemnly processed into the servants' hall and were then seated according to their status within the household. At Badminton Charles Dean remembered that the juniors had to be in their place at the table at least five minutes before the arrival of the seniors:

'as they approached we stood smartly to attention. After the meat course there were three divisions ...; the butler. housekeeper, valet and ladies' maids went to the pug's parlour, and the housemaids to their sitting-room. The meal was served and eaten in absolute silence'.

Only when the senior staff had departed was there a lighter mood, as the juniors ate the rest of their meal in a more relaxed atmosphere.

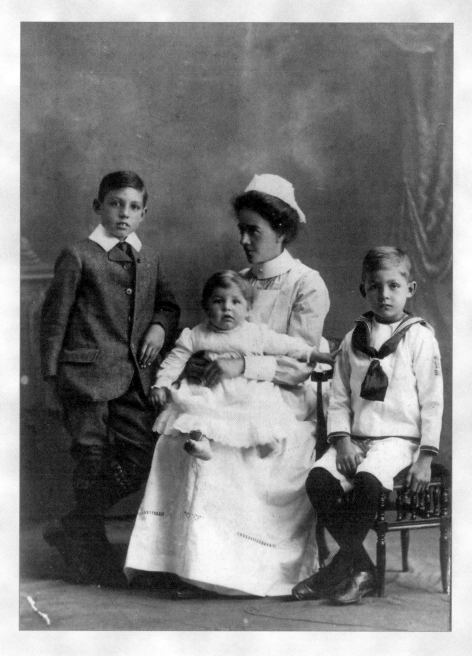

Figure 8. Nurse Abberley with three members of the Irving family in Wales c.1904. (Mr. E. J. B. Irving).

In-house promotions in such households were relatively rare, largely because they were considered likely to cause jealousy and ill-feeling among the rest of the staff. But occasionally some did take place. At Nuneham Park, William Hancock, one of the footmen, was promoted to valet in 1866, with a rise in pay from £27 6s. a year to £45. A year later his wages rose to £50 a year, and he remained in the household until the spring of 1871. His successor, John Sinden, was promoted to house steward in the summer of 1872, a position he held for over five years.[14] At Erddig near Wrexham, Harriet Rogers, the daughter of the estate carpenter, began her domestic career as a nursery maid. She then succeeded her sister as nanny, before moving on to become a lady's maid and eventually the cook-housekeeper. After she retired, Harriet remained close to the estate until her death in 1914.

But William Lanceley, who rose from hall-boy to house steward, noted sourly that in-house promotions not only created bad feeling but could encourage trickery. 'I have known cases where servants have let another down in order to chance their dismissal. Some will throw out hints in the hearing of their employers in regard to their conduct or carelessness over their work. This sort of thing comes mostly from men-servants who like their situation, but want to be doing better and have not the pluck to try a new situation.'[15] In-house promotions were thought to encourage such stratagems.

The Daily Round of the Female Servants

Indoor domestic service was dominated by females during the nineteenth and twentieth centuries and the most numerous group among them were the maids-of-all-work. The multiple duties they were expected to perform could lead to their becoming household drudges. Mrs. Milgate, who spent most of her working life as a housemaid in large households, went as a maid-of-allwork on two occasions. 'One I went out within a few days and the other after two weeks ... In that sort of job you never finished'.

Mrs. Beeton considered that the general servant was perhaps 'the only one of her class deserving of commiseration', adding that she had 'to rise with the lark, for she has to do in her own person all the work which in larger establishments is performed by cook, kitchenmaid, and housemaid, and occasionally the part of a footman's duty, which consists in carrying messages.' J. H. Walsh, in his *Manual of Domestic Economy*, agreed, describing the maid-of-all-work as 'the general drudge' who 'must be prepared to do everything in order, and yet be ready at a minute's notice to do anything else that is wanted by any member of the family.'

Naturally the duties varied with the circumstances of each household, but the diaries of Hannah Cullwick give an idea of what they could entail. Hannah first went to service in 1841 when she was aged eight, in her native Shropshire. After moving around a good deal, in 1869 she was recruited as a general servant by a middle-class widow and her daughter in London. Her fellow servants were a house-parlourmaid and a young hall boy. Because he was very small, Hannah had to do many of the jobs which would normally have fallen to him, such as carrying the coal or any heavy boxes that came to the house, as well as cleaning the high windows: 'anything as wants strength or height I am sent for ... to do it. All the cabs that's wanted I get, & if the young ladies want fetching or taking anywhere I've to walk with them & carry their cloaks or parcels.' In addition, she cleaned all the copper coal scuttles and helped with the silver. There was also washing up, and carrying 'things up as far as the door for dinner.' On 1 January, 1871 she described her typical routine:

'I clean 4 grates & do the fires & clean the irons, sweep & clean 3 rooms & my attic, the hall & front steps & the flags and area railings & all that in the street. I clean the water closet & privy... & the back yard & the area, the back stairs & the passage, the larder, pantry & boy's room & the kitchen & scullery, all the cupboards downstairs & them in the storeroom ... I get all the meals down stairs & lay the cloth & wait on the boy & the housemaid as much as they want ... I seldom get out of a weekday. I go with notes or parcels, & fetch my beer or for any errands ... The most fresh air is washing the front door steps & flags in the street & out at the back door washing the yard.[16]

Hannah was physically strong and she took pride in her domestic skills. Yet her experience was not unique, as the reminiscences of other maids confirm. Even in the 1920s conditions could be harsh. When young Minnie Cowley was engaged as a general servant at Richmond Hill in London she was paid 7s. 6d. a week, but as her mistress had provided part of her uniform, she had to pay for this at the rate of 2s. 6d. a week, which was deducted from her earnings. Once a week, in rotation, each room had to be turned out and thoroughly cleaned. There was no vacuum cleaner for the carpets, so tea leaves were sprinkled over them while they were damp, and then swept off with a hand broom. 'The big windows had to be cleaned, fireplaces blackleaded and tiles washed and polished, loads of silver polished ... Every morning the kitchen range had to be raked out and the fire lit; then it was blackleaded, the fender cleaned with emery cloth and the hearth hearthstoned. Finally the front step was swept and cleaned and the breakfast laid. All this was before the cook arrived at eight o'clock.' In the afternoons one of Minnie's chores was to take out her mistress's small son.[17]

Mrs. Beeton optimistically concluded that a 'bustling and active girl' engaged in a general servant's place would find time in the afternoon or evening for a little needlework for herself, provided she lived with 'consistent and reasonable people'. The available evidence casts doubt on this. In these circumstances the bitter comments of Ethel Sims in 1945 are perhaps understandable, when she wrote:

> 'I don't mind saying that there isnt *anything* that I wouldn't do to prevent *my* daughter ... entering domestic service. *I* had fourteen years in domestic service ... You are expected to call somebody the same age as yourself *Master* & *Mistress* ... If you have a half day you must leave tea laid in the drawing-room & dinner all laid in the dining room & when you return at *ten* pm you had to fill the hot water bottles, turn down the beds & then start to wash up all those tea and dinner things'.[18]

The variety of tasks expected from a general servant in a small household was in marked contrast to the situation in large establishments, where each member of staff had his or her allotted duties to perform, under the supervision of a senior servant.

At the head of the female staff was the housekeeper, or in smaller households the cook-housekeeper. She was expected to keep order among her underlings and could be an awesome figure. Eric Horne claimed she was more feared by the maids than was their mistress. The large bunch of household keys she carried was a symbol of her authority, and she and the cook were always referred to as 'Mrs', irrespective of their marital status, as a mark of respect. At Englefield House, the housekeeper was exhorted to 'provide for the Family of 16 to 20 servants ... & not let the Maids go out without your leave, & to take care that they are dressed quietly'.[19]

In addition to directing the female servants the housekeeper oversaw the contents of the linen cupboard and the china closet, as well as the stillroom, where cordials and preserves were made and stored, and cakes and scones produced for afternoon tea. The stillroom maids, working under her direction, prepared the early morning tea trays, too. At Longleat the Marchioness of Bath remembered the housekeeper performing 'feats of alchemy, distilling rose water from dark damask roses, producing pot-pourri from an old family recipe, preserving fruits, making jam, candying peel, bottling morello cherries in brandy, drying lavender to keep the linen cupboard sweet, and forever harrying the stillroom maids'. The staircase which wound up to the housekeeper's room was redolent with the smell of the stillroom itself, 'that delicious combination of hot bread, biscuits, coffee and herbs'.

In consultation with her mistress, the housekeeper allocated the bedrooms when visitors and their servants were expected. If she placed orders on behalf of the household - something which the cautious Mr. Benyon did not permit at Englefield - or she paid bills, these were recorded in a special account book, which the employer inspected. At Nuneham Courtenay, for example, in January 1884 the outgoings listed ranged from settling tradesmen's bills to the payment of 1s 6d to 'sweep for library', 1s for glue, and 2s 6d a day to a washerwoman, as well as small sums for stamps, paper and envelopes.[20]

Stores were distributed to the servants at regular intervals, and this, too, was the housekeeper's responsibility. At Shugborough during the 1930s the housekeeper, Mrs. Courtenay, remembered the weekly 'store days' as hectic, with the household linen, the 'general working stores as well as the food stores' given out.[21] But she was proud of her role: 'I devoted my whole life to it. I was so interested and I was so happy... I never bothered going out much after I was housekeeper'.

The housekeeper's day began when she went to the stillroom to oversee the giving out of the breakfast china and to check on the stillroom maids. At 8 am she presided over breakfast for the senior servants, after which she again went to the stillroom. Later she made a round of the bedrooms to see that all was in order. Often there were wider responsibilities, too, such as helping her mistress dispense charity to the neighbouring poor or taking charge of the house while the family was away. But always she would consult her mistress when there were decisions to be made. At Highclere Castle in 1839 Lord Carnarvon's long-serving housekeeper, Mrs. Gaymour, then in her mid-sixties, even wrote to her mistress to enquire whether she should preserve strawberries as the weather had been bad 'and all last year's remain'. She also enquired about the purchase of extra baby linen to be loaned to poor families.[22] At Bulstrode Park, Buckinghamshire, correspondence between Sir John Ramsden and his housekeeper, Mrs Dee, in the early 1890s reveals that she had to ask him to order such minor items as soda, soap and candles.

Normally the housekeeper was the highest paid female member of staff, although her male counterpart, the steward or the butler, usually earned more. But there were exceptions. At Nuneham Courtenay, Mrs. Kibblewhite was appointed housekeeper in May 1882 at £65 per annum. That was the same rate as the butler. However, by 1884 she was receiving £85 a year compared to the £70 per annum received by the then butler. This probably caused strains within the household for she left early in 1885. Significantly, her successor during most of the 1890s, Sarah Lewis, received £75 per annum, the same rate of pay as the butler. Some housekeepers were able to supplement their income with tips, especially in the eighteenth and early nineteenth centuries, by showing tourists round a stately home, especially if the family was away.

Ladies' maids occupied the next rung of the household ladder, but were only employed in the homes of the wealthy. In smaller establishments, a housemaid would carry out some of the duties of the lady's maid. Frequently they were from a superior background, and had received a prior training in dressmaking and hairdressing. The Harcourt family records show that three of the applicants for the post of lady's maid at Nuneham Courtenay in the late nineteenth century were respectively the daughters of a cashier in a timber merchant's office, a city clerk, and a gamekeeper on a Scottish estate. They also had a firm sense of the duties that befitted their station. One applicant announced she was leaving her current post because she had 'to set nursery tea, & take a great Dog out every day'.[23]

The fashion conscious particularly sought French or Swiss lady's maids, the former being preferred on account of their vivacity and superior dressmaking skills. A lady's maid had to be prepared to dress, undress and re-dress her mistress as often as the engagements of the day required. Other duties included laundering delicate articles of clothing in her mistress's wardrobe and preparing beauty preparations. She had to be an expert at packing and unpacking for country house visits and trips further afield. Rosina Harrison, when employed by Lady Cranborne, accompanied her mistress to Paris fashion shows, so that she could note the latest designs when carrying out her own dressmaking for her mistress. Later, when working for Lady Astor, she was responsible for looking after valuable jewellery. She recalled, too, that when her mistress returned from any sporting activity she would take a bath and then 'always slung her clothes into the bath ... I suppose she wanted to make certain they were washed each time.' [24] When Lady Astor went out in the evening, like all lady's maids, Rosina had to sit up to await her return, so that she could help her prepare for bed.

Lady's maids were often close to their employer and this could make them unpopular with other members of staff, who disliked the airs many of them assumed and suspected them of tale-bearing. One man, who worked at Sudeley Castle in the late 1920s, claimed that the lady's maid was 'easily the most hated servant of all... This was so in most big houses. Nothing escaped her eyes and her tongue wagged unceasingly.' Some lady's maids inherited their mistress's discarded clothes but when Mary Anne Disraeli appointed a maid in April 1845, she noted carefully that 'no clothes [were] promised.[25] Mrs. Disraeli's lady's maids also acted as housekeeper.

The cook, the third of the senior servants, was found in a wide range of households, and displayed a variety of skills. There was a great difference between the dishes produced by a 'plain' cook working in a two- or three-servant household and those of the 'professed' cook in a large establishment. In the wealthiest families a male chef would be employed. Occasionally families sent their female cooks to receive extra training. Mrs. Charles Brocklebank recalled that it was possible 'to send one's cook to somewhere like the Ritz or the Berkeley [hotels], where they could watch a particular dish being made'.[26]

Upon the cook's competence depended a family's reputation for hospitality. She was usually assisted by kitchenmaids and a scullery-maid and it was their duty to come down early in the morning to light the fire and clean the kitchen ready for the cook to begin work. In some households the senior kitchenmaid prepared and cooked the meals for the servants' hall while the cook concentrated on preparations for those 'above stairs'. In the hot, poorly ventilated atmosphere of the kitchen the cook and her assistants had to work very hard, and it was in conditions conducive to the intake of liquor that some cooks earned a reputation for drunkenness. Most also expected to have perquisites, dripping. rabbit skins, old tea-leaves and the like - which they sold to dealers for personal profit.[27]

However, the issue annoyed cost-conscious employers, who thought their cooks were over-lavish. In 1912 Alice Slater, a cook at Lord Rosebery's Scottish seat of Dalmeny, indignantly refuted the agent's accusation that she was guilty of 'extravagance & waste ... I have every bit of Everything used up to advantage, all bones are even stewed down to make Glaze to make the Sauces & gravies ... for his Lordship. Nothing is allowed to go bad & I fed twice as many people last month as were fed in the corresponding month last year'.[28] But the reprimands continued and Alice eventually left.

Menus were agreed with the mistress or the housekeeper, but any unannounced visits by these to the kitchen were not welcome. During the morning the dishes required for luncheon would be prepared, but it was in the early evening that the serious business of the day began. Between 5 pm and 8 pm was always a very busy time. Dishing up a large dinner with many courses was a responsible task. Once the dinner had been served the cook's duties for the day were over and the rest of the kitchen work was carried out by the kitchenmaids and the scullery-maid. This was not easy, for a full-length dinner for eighteen persons could produce as many as five hundred separate items to be washed up afterwards.

Girls hired as kitchenmaids or 'between maids' ('tweenies'), working partly as housemaids and partly as kitchenmaids in small households, were the drudges of this category of servants. They prepared the food for the cook, carried out all the pounding and chopping and, often enough, the staff cooking, as well as the washing up and scrubbing. They were frequently bullied by the cooks, too. A girl who worked in the scullery of Horsenden Manor in Buckinghamshire during the 1930s remembered preparing the vegetables and the poultry and game. 'I could skin, pluck and clean most animals, rabbits, rooks, poultry, pheasants, and the fish from the moat tossed, still flapping, in to me through the scullery window... I flatly refused though on one occasion, to skin a well hung hare that was heaving ... with maggots.' The cook would not allow her into the kitchen when she was working, so she peeped through the keyhole to see what was going on.[29] Another youngster who went as a kitchenmaid in 1939 recalled her chapped arms, which were the result of immersing them in bowls of water, some with soda, for the constant washing up.

One of the most common category of servants after the maid-of-all-work was the housemaid. It was her responsibility to keep the home clean and orderly and that was not easy, given the cluttered state of many Victorian and Edwardian rooms. In small establishments the housemaid also carried out certain of the duties of a parlourmaid, such as laying the table for meals, waiting at table, answering the door to callers, and announcing visitors. She might act as a lady's maid, too.

In well-to-do homes, where several housemaids were employed, the head maid would supervise the work of her underlings as well as perhaps dusting the ornaments and cleaning the furniture in the principal rooms. Margaret Thomas recalled that in one large house where she worked in Yorkshire, the fourth housemaid worked entirely for her fellow servants, the third was employed in the schoolroom, and the second performed general duties. She had to be downstairs by 4 am each morning to get the sitting-room in order before breakfast. 'The second housemaid had a medal room to keep clean ... The head housemaid did light jobs. They all did sewing'. At Shugborough, where early hours were also the order of the day, this meant that in winter much work was done in the dark, using a candle lamp kept in the housemaid's cleaning box. That was considered safer for them than having an oil lamp. The cleaning of the downstairs rooms had to be completed before 8 am when the family might be up and about. Wooden floors were dry-swept and dusted every day, and each pile of dust was checked by the housemaid to make sure she had not swept up anything of value. At 8 am the maids took off their soiled aprons and donned clean ones before collecting trays of tea to take to the family and their guests. Bedrooms were tidied while the family was at breakfast, with slops removed. That included emptying the chamber pot into the slop bucket. Fireplaces were cleaned and polished, ashes removed and the fire was laid or lit.[30] Much of this involved heavy physical labour, as a former footman conceded. 'Up at five to clean and light the fires, to polish the steel grates ... to whiten the hearths and later to take up the brass cans of hot water to the bedrooms. We men only started at seven and could sit down in the afternoons, but the girls had to darn and repair the linen - and all for eight pounds a year'.[31] That sum was being paid shortly before the First World War.

In the evening the housemaids prepared the bedrooms, including turning down the beds, filling the jugs with water, closing the curtains and taking up a can of hot water for each person to wash. When the family went down to dinner they made a round of the bedrooms and put them in order. In the drawing-room, newspapers and magazines were straightened and the fire grate tidied, so that all was ready for the family to return after dinner.

Parlourmaids were kept in place of footmen in some households, and J. H. Walsh applauded the move, considering that if they were 'of a suitable height and gifted with ordinary intelligence' they waited at table better than most men. They had the added merit, too, of being able to assist the housemaid. Some had extra responsibilities. Marion Sambourne entrusted her parlourmaid with the paying of bills and on at least one occasion she escorted Marion's difficult mother-in-law to the railway station when she was going away.[32]

Most servant-keeping families with children would seek to employ a nursemaid. Often these were quite young girls. Only in large establishments was the head nurse held in awe. She ran her own department quite separately from the rest of the household, and some women used their authority to make the lives of both their charges and their subordinates miserable. At Kingston Lacy Viola Bankes remembered that a sadistic nanny, Nurse Stanley, deprived the children of food and punished them at every opportunity. She scolded one of the nursemaids from morning to night for being too slow and the girl would stand weeping silently as Nurse Stanley threatened her with dismissal. Viola's widowed mother was bullied by the nanny, too, and it was only when the son and heir to the estate became seriously ill that a consultant was called in and the nanny's mistreatment of the children was exposed.[33]

Only a tiny minority of nannies displayed this kind of brutal authoritarianism and where parents were indifferent or neglectful, a nurse might be the only adult to provide affection and stability in the children's lives. This was true of the Sitwells of Renishaw in Derbyshire, and especially of the daughter, Edith. The nanny, Davis, was the only reliable and loving person in the little girl's life, at a time when her parents treated her with persistent disapproval.

Most head nurses were snobbish and would not allow 'their' children to mix with the offspring of families they considered inferior. But when appropriate, parties were organised, and nursery staff might also take their young charges on a seaside holiday while the parents pursued their own interests.

Sarah Sedgwick, who advanced from nursery maid to nanny, recalled there were dancing classes, too, where the children met their friends, and they also learnt to ride ponies. The nursemaids looked after the children's clothes and that was not easy at a time when they 'never wore the same clothes in the morning as they wore in the afternoon', and when there was 'a complete change from top to bottom when the dressing-up to go downstairs' to spend time with their parents in the drawing-room took place. As Sarah ruefully recalled: 'I was supposed to be in bed myself at 9.30, but that was something which could not always happen, ... for with the washing, ironing, and running in of ribbons I couldn't get done in time.' [34]

Most nannies worked their way up from nursery maids, as Sarah did. However, in the 1890s the Norland Training Institution (later College) for nursery nurses was opened in Notting Hill Gate, London. It aimed to recruit middle-class girls and to underline their superior status, employers who hired them had to agree that they would not be expected to eat with the ordinary domestic staff. They were also to wear the distinctive college uniform when on duty. In the early twentieth century other training establishments were set up. But the number of graduates employed in the nation's nurseries remained small.

The final category of female servants, the laundrymaids, were, like the nanny and the housekeeper, hired by the richest families only. The laundry itself comprised a wash-house, an ironing room, and a drying room, sometimes supplemented by a drying-closet heated by a furnace. It was usually separated from the house because of the damp and steam, with the laundrymaids receiving board wages, so they could cater for themselves. In some households other members of staff were called upon to help the laundrymaids, or part-time workers were hired. Large establishments despatched washing from the family's London house to be laundered on the country estate, it being sent by train in hampers. The clean washing was returned in a similar fashion. By 1893, indeed, the Duke of Devonshire's Chatsworth had an up-to-date laundry which received washing not only from the family's town house but from some of their other residences.

Individual skills were prized when fine fabrics were being laundered, and some laundresses were highly paid. At Nuneham Courtenay in the second half of the 1870s the head laundress was paid £75 and £80 per annum, while the then housekeepers received £50 or £60 a year. But many of the tasks required teamwork, especially when large sheets and heavy curtains had to be handled. Long hours spent ironing were eased by companionable gossip and songs.

Despite the laborious nature of the work, the fact that the laundry was located away from the main house gave the workers an opportunity to strike up clandestine relationships. Barbara Charlton of Hesleyside in Northumberland was shocked to learn, years later, that the mid-century laundry was 'nothing but a brothel until a new entrance was built and gates put up to keep intruders out'.[35]

By the end of the nineteenth century the number of families with estate laundries had declined sharply. They preferred the cheaper alternative of sending their washing out, or perhaps they relied on a weekly washerwoman coming to the house to do the laundry. A few families did continue the old tradition and even in 1890 the Harcourts had a laundry at Nuneham Courtenay in full operation, with a wages bill of about £107 5s per annum. Mentmore, too, had its laundry in the early twentieth century, although the agent drew Lord Rosebery's attention to the heavy outlay on coal this entailed.[36]

The Daily Round of the Male Servants

The role of male servants in private households differed from that of the females in three important respects. First, unlike the women, their numbers fell during the nineteenth century, and particularly during the final thirty years of that century, when totals dropped from 68,369 in 1871 to 47,893 in 1901, according to the census returns. Second, they were found only in the households of the well-to-do or those who aspired to gentility. At the end of the nineteenth century a new edition of Mrs. Beeton's *Book of Household Management* commented drily that young pages and hall-boys were kept 'more for appearance than anything else, some people preferring to see a boy open the door or wait at table to women servants doing these duties'. But it warned that 'Boys [were] proverbially tiresome', wasting time if sent on an errand and not always ready to answer the door. A 'neat parlour-maid' was an 'excellent substitute'. [37]

The third difference between male and female servants was that while the womenfolk had to provide their own uniforms, the men were normally supplied with clothing or with a clothes allowance. In the case of under-butlers and footmen, who wore livery, the provision could be generous. For example, at Nuneham Courtenay in the early 1880s - and typically - these servants received two suits of livery each year, plus one working suit, dress livery for special occasions as required, a great coat every three or four years, hats and gloves .[38] House stewards and butlers did not wear livery but often had a cash allowance in lieu. They wore the gentlemen's clothes of the period distinguished by a deliberate solecism, such as the wrong tie or the wrong trousers, to mark their status as servants.

Yet while wealthy households had their hierarchy of male staff, headed by a house steward or butler, a large proportion of resident males were employed in a single-handed capacity alongside a small female staff. Around a third of them were very young, being under twenty. Many were the masculine counterpart of the maid-of-all-work. They included the Suffolk lad, Robert Savage, who worked on a prosperous farm in his home village as a kitchen boy. His duties ranged from lighting fires, cleaning knives and boots, chopping wood for fuel and filling the coal scuttles, to feeding the poultry, collecting eggs and carrying out other farming chores. In the towns, hall-boys or kitchen boys did not have such a wide range of tasks as country lads like Robert Savage, but they spent more time running errands, taking messages, answering the front door to callers, and accompanying their mistress when she went out, as an adult footman would do.

Advertisements in the newspapers indicate the kind of duties expected of these youngsters, such as the appeal for a 'Strong respectable Lad, about 18, to look after pony and trap, garden, clean knives and boots and make himself generally useful'. This appeared in the *Hampshire Chronicle* in 1890 but it was characteristic of the requirements for boy servants in the national and provincial press during the Victorian years.

In more affluent households an adult single-handed manservant would be recruited. Usually he would be out of livery and would work alongside two or three maids. He rose early enough to complete the heavier or rougher tasks of the day before breakfast, such as getting in coal and wood, before dressing himself to serve the family. Often he acted as valet to the male head of the household and would carry up cans of hot water for family baths.

He laid the breakfast and carried in the food for the family, although he did not normally wait at this meal, as he did at luncheon and dinner. During the morning he cleared the breakfast things away and washed and replaced them in the pantry. He trimmed the lamps and cleaned the silver, which could be a laborious task. Other duties included attending to the sitting-room fires, answering the bell, and opening the door to callers. Sometimes he went out with the carriage when his mistress went for a drive, or he waited for her outside shops while she made purchases. At night he made sure that the doors and windows of the house were secured and the fires

Figure 9. John Henry Inch, a butler at Marlands, Itchingfield, Horsham with his two footmen, c.1922. (Arthur R. Inch).

safe. Other miscellaneous chores included cleaning windows, mirrors and chandeliers, moving furniture around and, most importantly, running errands and taking messages. That might even mean carrying messages to other family members within the house itself. Some, like the single-handed London footman, William Tayler, paid bills and received commission from tradespeople in return. On 12 April, 1837, Tayler noted in his diary: 'Went this morning to pay a bill. The tradesman gave me half a crown - that was better than nothing'. When dinner parties were held at the house he hoped to receive tips but these were not always as generous as he desired. On 9 March he recorded ruefully: 'Had company to dinner and more to tea. I got one shilling out of the whole lot. It's quite out of fashion to give anything to servants at such times'.[39] In large households the situation was different. There senior servants in particular would expect to gain a valuable addition to their income from tips.

William Tayler worked for Mrs. Prinsep, a well-to-do widow and her middle-aged daughter, along with three women servants. Although his daily routine followed the traditional lines of a single-handed servant, he was able to find time to pursue his own leisure interests, such as reading magazines and painting pictures during the afternoons when he was not required to do more than open the door to visitors and take up tea trays, as well as lamps and candles to the drawing-room during the winter months, or make up the fire. Sometimes he went out with the carriage and made clear his displeasure when this seemed to last too long, as it did on 19 May, 1837. On that occasion he had accompanied Miss Prinsep: 'She kept me out longer than she aught to of done, therefore I gave her a little row for it. I hope it will do her good. I served the old lady the same way the other day and it did her a deal of good'.

Only the richest families employed the full range of male servants. It was here that the house steward, the butler, the valet and the chef practised their skills and supervised the activities of the footmen, pages, and odd-job men - usually labelled 'odd men'.

The house steward was the most senior member of the domestic staff and worked in the most prestigious establishments. His responsibilities could include, as at Lord Leconfield's estate of Petworth in Sussex, paying monthly bills which in the 1890s totalled the large sum of £1,000. He controlled the purchases and hired extra staff when required. He also arranged such minor matters as the sweeping of chimneys, the tuning of pianos and the winding of the multiplicity of clocks.[40]

The steward was expected to supervise the migrations of the family and their servants from one residence to another. That included the packing and safe transit of valuable items, like the family plate. When a steward was employed, the senior servants ate in his room, rather than with the housekeeper and if there were visitors he would escort into dinner the visiting lady's maid whose mistress was of the highest rank.

Butlers and under-butlers were more widely employed than stewards. The butler's duties varied with the wealth and status of his master or mistress. The larger the number of underlings he had the greater were his administrative responsibilities but the lighter his practical duties. These could mostly be offloaded to an under-butler or the footmen.

The butler superintended the serving of meals and the preparation of the dining-table. He was responsible for the household plate and each night would make sure it was carefully locked away. He would look after the wine cellar, keeping a record of the bottles that were taken out and used, and when fresh purchases were made. If there were no valet the butler would be responsible for his master's wardrobe and that could be an arduous task if his master were a hunting man. John Henry Inch, employed as a butler at Nidd Hall in Yorkshire during the 1920s and early 1930s, is remembered by his son as staying up until midnight on some occasions to clean his master's white leather hunting breeches. 'I often used to watch him polishing these leather breeches until I'm sure his hands must have been very sore and he dog tired. His Lordship also had a pheasant shoot on the estate and my father had to go out as his loader, tramping over ploughed fields all day carrying heavy bags of cartridges and a 12-bore shotgun ... Then having to return after these shoots and serve a dinner starting at 8 pm and if there were guests could go on till ten, eleven or midnight'.[41] He accompanied his employer, Viscount Mountgarret, to a shooting lodge in Scotland, where deer stalking and salmon fishing were the order of the day, and might stay away from home for six to eight weeks.

Advertisements in the press give a flavour of what was expected, as in *The Field* of 2 January, 1886, when an unmarried twenty-nine-year-old offered his services as a butler, and valet if necessary: 'twelve months and eight years excellent character; understands hunting, shooting, and fishing things'.

In large country mansions these various tasks could involve a great deal of walking. Between the two World Wars the Duke of Richmond and Gordon remembered attaching a pedometer to the elderly butler, and being shocked to discover that in one day he had walked nineteen and a half miles. 'He died with us; overwork I should think'.[42]

The office of butler was normally one which not only commanded respect but ensured the smooth running of the household. At Kingston Lacy, Viola Bankes remembered Cooper, the butler, as the 'keystone' of the whole establishment. He 'perfected the training of the other servants' and was himself 'a treasure beyond words ... always dressed in black, he was the perfect butler in every word and gesture'. Like most butlers he looked after the family plate and was 'an authority on all the wine in the cellars'. He showed off the Bankes family's collection of valuable pictures to visitors, doled out the children's pocket money, and played billiards and cricket with them when their mother was away from home:

> 'Nothing ever went wrong with the smooth running of the household during the time that Cooper was our butler ... He slept in a comfortable room ... next to the muniment room ... and near a cellar where the silver was kept. Beside him lay a long, inlaid revolver'. [43]

Presumably he had the firearm to frighten off potential burglars.

Edwin Lee, who worked at Cliveden, was another butler paragon, whose responsibilities in the 1920s and 1930s were particularly onerous because of the Astors' involvement in politics, and the fact that there were weekly migrations between Cliveden and their London house. One of the footmen who worked under him described Lee as the 'highest skilled professional butler I've ever met ... a word of praise from him would keep a man happy for a week'. But he felt the weight of his responsibilities, declaring years later that he had felt like 'a captain of a ship, there was no one to whom I could go with my problems'.[44] He resented Lady Astor interfering when he was hiring footmen, noting on one occasion that her intervention had prevented the appointment of a suitable candidate and that he had given her 'a piece of my mind', but 'she couldn't learn'.

Not all butlers reached these high standards. The ready access to alcohol turned a number of them into drunkards. Ernest King in his first place as hall-boy on a Devon estate remembered that when his master and mistress went out for the day, the butler would go down to the cellar and ring the bell to summon all the stable hands, gardeners and estate workers: 'Come on, boys,' he would cry, 'another b— anniversary.' And the beer would flow. Perhaps not surprisingly he eventually died of drink, according to King.[45] It was to prevent this that cautious employers like Richard Benyon at Englefield kept the key to their own cellar and doled out supplies as and when they thought fit.

The groom of the chambers was akin in status to the butler, but was found only in the largest houses, where his role was largely ceremonial. His duties included receiving and announcing visitors and showing guests to their rooms. Several times a day he toured his domain, adjusting blinds against the sun, patting cushions, straightening chairs, placing footstools and checking on the supplies of notepaper. He performed much door opening and at meals was expected to help with the serving. At Wilton he also acted as his master's valet, but a daughter of the household recalled dismissively that his main duties seemed to comprise cleaning pens, replacing blotting paper on the writing tables, and putting water on them, presumably for the sealing of envelopes.

The footman was the male servant most directly subordinate to the butler and was expected to perform various duties, ranging from attending his employer in the carriage to cleaning knives and boots, carrying coal, cleaning plate, looking after the lamps and candle-holders, waiting at table and answering the bell. Where an under-butler was kept, he would be responsible for cleaning the silver, but whoever carried this out, in a wealthy household it was a laborious task. Ernest King remembered learning the rudiments from a footman when he worked as a hall-boy. It involved the use of a special rouge powder, mixed in a saucer with ammonia. The resultant paste was then applied by hand. 'Cleaning plate is hell... When I began this work, rubbing the silver, ... my fingers grew fearfully sore and blistered, but ... if you complained you were just told to get on with it'. The blisters burst and eventually 'you developed a pair of plate hands that ... became as hard as boards'.

An efficient footman rose early so as to complete the dirtiest jobs before the family came down. He then put aside his working dress, tidied himself and appeared in a clean jacket to lay the cloth and prepare the breakfast table for the family. Among the tasks carried out by John Henry Inch in the 1890s, when he was working as a footman in a stately home in Devon, was ironing copies of *The Times* into four folds before they went through to the front of the house. If there were male visitors without their own valets, the footman performed some of those duties, brushing clothes, laying them out ready for wear, and providing water for washing.

At midday a footman had to be dressed in his livery, ready to answer the door, take messages, or carry out any other chores required. Both employers and servants prided themselves on the. livery. Eric Horne recalled that when he was employed by a man whom he called 'the Baron' he and his fellow footman had to 'help in the buffet, and ... go round every two hours and wind up the ... colza oil lamps, also watch the candles' when a ball was being held during the London Season. 'The Baron was fond of pomp and show,' wrote Horne, 'and liked to see his dress liveries walking about.' He remembered, too, the long hours servants were on duty during the Season. Sometime's he fell asleep the following day when on carriage duty, and had to be woken up by the coachman.[46] For special occasions some employers still wanted their footmen to powder their hair, although the men themselves disliked this because of the effect it had on their hair. Footmen were addressed by their Christian name, and there were households where the name was attached to a particular position, so that the first footman was always called Charles, the second James, and the third John, for example.[47] Mary Anne Disraeli noted in January 1845 when she appointed John Felton as 'lady's footman' that he was to be called James. He was paid £25 a year, plus £1 a year for hair powder, and when on board wages was to receive 12s a week.[48]

In the eighteenth and early nineteenth centuries, footmen had had protective duties to perform, at a time when policing was rudimentary and there was a good deal of street violence. But by the Victorian era that role had disappeared and their function was largely ceremonial. Where several footmen were employed, the first, or most senior of them, acted as the lady's footman, sitting on the box with the coachman when she went driving or in later years sitting beside the chauffeur, opening and shutting the door for her, and wrapping a fur rug around her knees. If she dined in her room, he carried up the tray and at the dinner table he stood behind her chair.

Footmen spent a good deal of time waiting around, especially when on carriage duty. In the late 1830s Thomas, footman to the second Duke of Sutherland, noted in his diary that he was ordered to go with the carriage to Buckingham Palace to collect the Duke from a ball at midnight. In practice his master did not leave until 3 am and Thomas stayed with the carriage until he was ready to depart. Often this aimless waiting led footmen and coachmen to go drinking in public houses or in the servants' hall of the house their master or mistress was visiting.[49]

The valet, like the groom of the chambers, was something of a status symbol and was normally only engaged in the richest households or as a general factotum by a bachelor. In other cases the butler or a footman filled the role. He did not wear livery but often received his master's cast-offs, which he could sell if he wished. Like the lady's maid, he enjoyed a close relationship with his employer, and surviving correspondence sheds light on what employers expected of their valets. In 1873, when Lord Carnarvon recruited a new man, it was noted that the successful candidate had previously served as valet and groom of the chambers to the Duke of Montrose, thereby indicating that he was familiar with High Society. He was used to looking after hunting and shooting clothes, was able to order 'anything in French', was unmarried and was 'sober, honest ... Steady with horses

& in all respects' a reliable servant. He was aged thirty-one. Proficiency in a foreign language and an ability to act as a courier when travelling abroad were an advantage for a valet, as well as skill in looking after his master's clothing, being able to pack and unpack speedily and efficiently, and make arrangements for rail journeys. That included being able to secure a reserved compartment. Even the hostile Lady Violet Greville admitted that a well-trained valet was useful. 'He never forgets a single portmanteau or bag or hat-box; ... Your boots are polished till you can see your face in them; ties are carefully arranged, clothes are ironed, and brushed hats are glossy; ... hot water is to your hand; your slippers lie in front of the fire ... If he smokes your cigars, your loose cash may lie about freely; he will not touch it ... If he occasionally helps himself to a glass or two of wine, he pays your bills punctually and in order ... The gentleman's gentleman ... is agreeable to live with, easy to manage, unobtrusively useful, faithful as far as his lights go'. Not all valets met these exacting standards, however. In at least one case in 1840 a young Swiss valet, Francois Courvoisier, murdered his elderly employer, Lord William Russell, seemingly after being provoked by his master's unreasonable demands and ill-temper.

The male cook or chef was recruited by the most affluent families and the hiring of a Frenchman for the position was considered especially desirable by gastronomes and the most status conscious. But they could be temperamental beings, who were hard on their underlings. At Shugborough between the Wars the French chef was remembered as a man of uncertain temper who expected his female kitchen staff to curtsey to him when he entered the kitchen in the morning. He and the female cook who worked alongside him each had a kitchenmaid. These girls had to have the table laid out with the appropriate equipment before their superiors arrived to begin work. According to one of the kitchenmaids the chef refused to move from the table: 'everything had to be within his reach'. The only exception was when he went into his own pantry to make pastry on the marble-topped table in there. This was perhaps to preserve the secrets of his art or merely to have a cold surface for the pastrymaking.

At late Victorian Longleat the chef was Albert Gaillard, who was a friend of the Royal chef at Buckingham Palace. He was assisted by two kitchenmaids, a vegetable maid, a scullery maid and a daily woman. When the family was in London he went to the Palace to help at big dinner parties, and in return the Palace chef came to the Marquis of Bath's residence to prepare some of his own specialities on important occasions. Gaillard, like all French chefs, was highly paid, receiving a salary of £130 a year in 1883. This may be compared to the £60 per annum paid to the Longleat housekeeper.

Apart from their uncertain temperament, chefs were often accused of extravagance by cost-conscious employers. At Petworth, for example, the house steward and Lord Leconfield himself specified that local suppliers should provide most of the food purchased for the household, but the chef was permitted to order extra delicacies, such as turtle soup, truffles and some spices on his own account. Outside his office there was a weighing room where supplies were checked on arrival to make sure they were correct before they were stored in the larder. The chef appointed the kitchen staff both at Petworth and at the London house, and hired extra cooks and charwomen when needed for special events.[50]

At Mentmore the agent lamented the extravagance of the newly-appointed French chef, M. Chevalier, in 1911. Purchases of food had risen from just over £1,576 in 1909 and a little less in 1910, to £2,057, while the cost of additional help in the kitchen had grown from a modest £66 in 1909 to £109 in 1911. In an attempt to curb his outgoings Chevalier was required to keep detailed accounts, but clearly this did not work for in February 1912 the agent wrote to Lord Rosebery to suggest that a woman cook be employed. She would work under the overall control of the steward. He conceded that major London dinners would have to be prepared by specially hired chefs, but as Chevalier was already hiring additional staff when necessary, 'I can't see why a woman could not do the same'. Rosebery was unenthusiastic, declaring coldly, 'hired chefs are simply appalling'. But by August 1912, in a letter which seemingly signified that he was departing, Chevalier had clearly grown tired of the reprimands, declaring sourly: 'really the place is too much trouble and not worth it'. At this time he was being paid £140 per annum, although that was £10 a year less than his immediate predecessor had received.[51]

Lady Violet Greville viewed the employment of a foreign chef with a jaundiced eye: 'he enjoys a wild liberty denied to the other servants, he stays out late ... Year by year Italians and Frenchmen invade our shores, and take possession of our kitchens, ... ruling obsequious kitchenmaids and scullions with a rod of iron'.[52] She doubtless shared the sentiments of Dr. Kitchiner when he declared: 'An English girl properly instructed can equal the best foreign gentlemen in everything except impudence and extravagance and send up a delicious dinner with half the usual expense and trouble.'[53] But in aristocratic circles the cachet of having a skilled foreign chef, able to enhance a family's reputation for first-class hospitality outweighed the disadvantages.

CHAPTER THREE
The Daily Round: Outdoor Workers

Landed Estates

The number and kind of outdoor servants employed on country estates varied according to their size and complexity and the wealth of the owner. Normally they included craftsmen and labourers on a home farm, as well as gardeners, foresters, stable staff and gamekeepers. The artisans carried out maintenance work on the estate and its cottages, in addition to shoeing the horses and providing fencing, gates, hinges and similar items. On large properties they were supervised by an estate agent, aided by a clerk of works, but for small establishments a foreman sufficed. At Erddig it was William Gittins who ruled the estate's building yard and joiner's shop for about forty years. He had twelve men working under him and his remit extended to organising the building of cottages, repairing walls and roads, and miscellaneous tasks like repairing furniture and making toys for the Yorke children. In 1911 Philip Yorke, his employer, praised his craftsmanship and versatility in rhyme.[1]

On most estates the number of outdoor workers exceeded those employed indoors, as at Eaton, where in the late nineteenth century the Duke of Westminster employed over three hundred men and women. Of these more than 250 worked out-of-doors. They included a clerk of works, with forty tradesmen and labourers under him; a head forester with seventy underlings; a head gardener with a staff of forty; and a head gamekeeper with six underkeepers. There were forty-one workers on the home farm, including a bailiff, and most of the remainder were in the stables or at the shire horse stud.

The Duke was immensely wealthy and could afford numerous servants, but even more modest establishments followed along similar,if more limited, lines. Indeed, as late as 1928 at Cliveden the Astors' nineteen indoor servants were more than matched by fifty-two employed outdoors, although some of these were part-timers. In addition, nineteen worked on Lord Astor's dairy farm on the other side of the Thames at Cookham, and eight were at the stud farm adjoining the main estate.[2]

At Cliveden and on many similar estates the workers and their families formed a distinct community, often dominating the population of a village.

Arthur Inch, whose father was butler on the Nidd estate in Yorkshire during the 1920s, remembered that the outdoor staff included two head gardeners (an unusual arrangement) and twelve under gardeners; two chauffeurs, of whom one not only kept the cars in good order but also looked after the dynamo which supplied electricity to Nidd Hall and nearby cottages; and several grooms. There were two gamekeepers and a hunt kennels with a head huntsman and two whips, while three or four foresters looked after the many wooded areas, as well as supplying fencing posts, stakes and logs for the open fires. A carpenter carried out the joinery work needed, while the blacksmith was kept busy shoeing the hunters and the farm horses. He also made iron tools, hinges and other items for use on the estate. A plumber and two painters worked there, too, and there was a Hall carter who carried out odd carting jobs. These included collecting the braces of dead pheasants during shoots.[3]

These men were often expected to carry out tasks beyond their basic trade, as the Duke of Richmond and Gordon recalled of Gordon North, the house carpenter at Goodwood: 'Gordon North ... made every single thing in the house. If one wanted anything one said, "Where's Gordon?" Gordon *was* Goodwood'.[4]

It was in such circumstances that in 1849 Sir Robert Peel, on a visit to Woburn Abbey, expressed astonishment at the size of the estate yard, considering its range of workshops 'more like a dockyard than a domestic office'.[5] At Petworth, too, the servants' block in Victorian times was compared to a factory production line:

Figure 10. Estate staff at Thame Park, Oxfordshire, home of the Wykeham-Musgrave family c.1900. (Centre for Oxfordshire Studies and Oxfordshire County Council Photographic Archive).

Food and other raw materials were delivered to the back door, and then stored and treated in a carefully planned series of larders, dairies and other service rooms until finally being prepared in the kitchens. At the opposite end, the business of the Estate was conducted in the estate offices, reached by a separate entrance and linked to the main house by a covered walkway. [6]

Apart from the many different categories into which outdoor workers were divided, they were distinguished from the indoor servants in several other ways. First and foremost they were predominantly male. Females were usually confined to the dairy, although a few might help in the gardens, usually part-time, as estate wages books show. Second, at a time when the number of male domestic servants was shrinking during the second half of the nineteenth century, the total of privately employed gardeners and gamekeepers was rising rapidly, especially in the late Victorian and Edwardian years. At a time when game preservation and shooting parties were increasingly popular, the number of gamekeepers grew from 12,633 in 1881 to 16,677 in 1901, a rise of almost a third. By 1911 they numbered 17,148, although the census report of that year considered this was an underestimate of the true position, because of a change in the system of classification. In 1911 there were also 118,739 domestic gardeners, up from 87,900 recorded in 1901.[7]

A third point of difference was that whereas indoor workers, especially in large households, frequently came from a distance away, it was common for many outdoor employees to be drawn from the locality. Only in the case of head gardeners and gamekeepers might this not apply, as advertisements in specialist trade publications like *The Gardeners' Chronicle* and *The Gamekeeper* confirm. Scots head gardeners were particularly popular among the Victorians, seemingly on account of their superior education and training.

Wages, too, were paid on a different basis, with outdoor staff usually receiving a simple cash sum, plus rent-free accommodation in many cases, while their indoor counterparts received part of their earnings in kind, in the form of board and lodging and perhaps free laundry plus, for the menfolk, free livery or a clothing allowance. However, where workers lived in estate cottages this could have its penalties, with employers laying down specific conditions, for example that candidates must be without children or have a wife available to work in the laundry or help in the house when required. Typical of this approach was an appeal in *The Gardeners' Chronicle* of 20 February, 1875 for a 'WORKING HEAD GARDENER, without children, thoroughly experienced, competent in the Management of Conservatory and Vines, and ordinary work. Must have a knowledge of Land and Stock. Wife should be able to Manage Poultry.' The proviso about children was fairly common and for this reason Joseph Addison, who was head gardener at Lyme Park in Cheshire between 1907 and 1922, considered himself fortunate to be appointed. He had five children and, according to his daughter, was 'worried he wouldn't get the job' on that account, even though he had had a successful career in more than one stately home before applying for the post at Lyme.[8]

The working hours of outdoor staff were normally more regular than was the case with their indoor colleagues and generally they stayed on the property for which they had been hired, unless they chose to move of their own accord. Only in the case of large landowners with a number of properties might that not be true, so that the young Chatsworth gardener, Robert Aughtie transferred in 1848 from the Duke of Devonshire's property in Chiswick to his prestigious Derbyshire estate.[9]

The relationship between outdoor servants and their employer also differed compared to that with indoor staff. The craft skills possessed by many of them and the fact that these often had a market value outside the sphere of personal service boosted their self-confidence and earned them a respect from their master or mistress which was given to few but the most senior domestic staff. On some estates the relationship between the head gardener or head gamekeeper and his employer was more like a partnership than one of master and servant, and the resultant warm feelings might result in a legacy when the employer died. Partly this stemmed from the fact that the skills of a head gardener could transform the surroundings of a house and thereby enhance its reputation, while in the case of a gamekeeper, his knowledge could ensure that shooting parties were a success. It was the flair of Joseph Paxton and his entrepreneurial abilities that largely made Chatsworth by the middle of the nineteenth century perhaps the most famous garden in the country, to the delight of his employer. The friendship between the 6th Duke of Devonshire and his gardener was made clear in a letter written by the Duke to Paxton: 'I had rather all the flowers in the garden were dead than you ill'. The high esteem in which the Duke held Paxton was also shown when he invited his head gardener to Bolton Abbey, his property in Yorkshire, for a shoot. It was a signal honour for an employee. By the mid-nineteenth century Paxton's authority had grown far beyond the confines of the garden and the pleasure grounds at Chatsworth. According to his biographer, he controlled all the accounts of the estate for land, farms, house and garden, as well as for the schools and villages owned by the Duke and other general disbursements and pensions. He was responsible, too, for the game, fisheries, annuities and taxes due from the property, land and mines. The sums under his control rose from around £9,000 a year to upward of £26,000, and his own pay advanced from £276 per annum to £500, plus an allowance for two assistants.[10]

Relations between the Duke of Devonshire and his head gardener were unusually close, but there were many other examples of friendships developing between master and servant in respect of outdoor workers. Lord Willoughby de Broke, for example, wrote warmly in his autobiography of the head gamekeeper at Compton Verney, Jesse Eales, praising him as 'not only the complete master of woodcraft ... but ... also a cultivated and versatile companion who could talk well on almost any subject. After my father and mother he was my first and my best friend ... It was with him that I saw my first fox killed; it was with him that I killed my first pheasant, partridge, duck, hare, rabbit and rook; also my first fish ... He had served my grandfather, and had performed all these good offices for my father and uncles'.[11]

The eccentric Sir Vauncey Harpur Crewe of Calke Abbey early in the twentieth century made his head gamekeeper, Agathos Pegg, his sole confidant. That included setting Pegg to spy on his daughter, Airmyne, whom he suspected of breaking his prohibition on smoking within the house.[12]

After the First World War economic pressures, rising taxes, and technological change all brought about a reduction in the number of workers on most estates. At Lyme Park one man felt that the purchase of motor vehicles had proved the beginning of the end for the old way of life. 'When the horses left, the wheelwright and the blacksmith left, and the "village" started to disintegrate'. These difficulties intensified during the world-wide depression of the late 1920s and early 1930s. At Petworth in 1931 the garden layout was simplified and the staff reduced from over thirty to sixteen. Since most married estate gardeners lived in a tied cottage, when they lost their employment they also lost their home, and many of the older men had difficulty in finding a fresh post. The situation was aggravated by the fact that until February 1937 private gardeners (like all other private servants) were excluded from the benefits of Unemployment Insurance. If they could not find a new job they might have to rely on poor relief, or its 1930s successor, public assistance, with its associated social stigma. Other privately employed workers, such as gamekeepers, ghillies, grooms and stable men similarly remained outside the unemployment scheme until 1938. Only if they worked in commercial concerns, such as hotels, were they covered from the beginning of the 1920s, like most other manual workers.

On some properties surplus garden produce was sold to local shops or even to Covent Garden to generate additional income. This had occurred on a small scale in the nineteenth century, as garden account books confirm, but after 1918 it became more general. At Nidd Hall the butler's son, Arthur Inch, remembered

SMALL ADVERTISEMENTS.

IMPORTANT NOTICE!—The proprietor of the Shooting Times begs to inform Advertisers and others that he cannot accept any responsibility for the *trustworthiness* of either those who advertise in these columns or those who answer the advertisements. It is most advisable for gentlemen having transactions with individuals who are strangers to them to insist upon the money for the goods being placed in the hands of some reliable and independent person who will not part with the cash until the sale is satisfactorily concluded or abandoned.

Situations Wanted and Vacant.

These Advertisements are inserted at the following scale:—20 WORDS, 1s., AND 6D. EXTRA FOR EACH 10 WORDS AFTERWARDS. Three insertions for the price of two. Replies addressed to the Office can be forwarded for 6d. extra. Prepayment in all cases necessary.

WANTED, situation as gamekeeper or rabbit catcher. Married. Thoroughly experienced. Apply William Mortlock. Blidworth. Mansfield. Notts.

WANTED, situation as gamekeeper or servant to sporting gentleman by single young man. Can train and fly hawks or falcons. Also good wildfowler. 13 years' character. Would not object going abroad. Apply D. T., Shooting Times Office, St. Bride's-avenue, Fleet-street, E.C.

KENNEL MAN.—Wanted, at once, thoroughly experienced single man, age 20 to 25, to take charge of show collies. Wages 18s. per week and lodgings. Apply by letter, stating age, experience, previous situation, and references, to H. W. Ethelston, Esq, Newbold, Revel, Rugby.

GAMEKEEPER, wants situation as single handed, or would take beat; thoroughly understands pheasant and partridge rearing and breaking young dogs; is a good ferreter and trapper, wirer of rabbits, and understands all duties of gamekeeper, or would take job rabbit catching; height, 5 ft. 10 in.; weight, 12 stone; strong and active; excellent character; please state wages. Address L Moseley, Hocksway, East Marden, Chichester, Sussex.

A GENTLEMAN wishes to recommend his keeper for head or single-handed. A good all round man, married with small family. Age 39. Height 5 ft.. 10 in., 12 stone. W. J., Shooting Times Office, St. Bride's-avenue, Fleet-street, E.C.

WANTED, by a strong active young man, a situation as under-gamekeeper. Age 24, height 5 ft 10 in., weight 12 stone. Apply C. Munt, Gamekeeper, Walton-in-Gordons, near Clevedon. Somerset.

AS ASSISTANT UNDER-KEEPER, by single man, age 27, height 5 ft 8 in., weight 12 stone; used to trapping vermin and wiring; can be recommended by a gentleman. Address J. J, 12 Chapel-place, Tunbridge Wells, Kent.

YOUNG MAN (21), son of a surgeon, pupilage just expired, wishes to meet with situation requiring assistant manager or general help. Can keep books and understands business. Salary not so much an object as comfortable home and further experience. Address H. N. Lacey, Park-lane House, Royston, Oldham, Lancashire

GAMEKEEPER.—A gentleman wishes to recommend his head keeper, who has a thorough practical knowledge of pheasant and partridge rearing, dog breaking etc; is a most respectable, reliable, honest man; age 30, married, with small family; wife capable of taking charge of lodge and opening gate. Apply N. Storey. Moor Park. Farnham.

AS GAMEKEEPER or rabbit catcher. Age 31, height 5 ft. 10 in. Strong and active. Good character. W. White, Coalpit-lane, Sittingbourne, Kent.

GUNMAKERS.—Salesman, etc. seeks situation, or as stocker. Knowledge of finishing and general work. Moderate salary. 28 February-street, Manchester,

Shootings and Fishings Wanted and To Let.

NORTH WALES.—To be let, furnished house seven bedrooms; warm and south aspect on sea coast; rabbit shooting; sea and river fishing; use of small yacht. Also a four-roomed cottage on the sands. Agent, Glasfryn, Chwilog N. Wales

4,000 ACRES of good mixed game. rabbit and wildfowl shooting, sea fishing, etc. Capital golf links adjoin hotel. Sporting course over dry fancy turf, and with the height and mild climate, give golfers and sportsmen a pleasant variety of amusement. Plan and inclusive tariff on request. Maelog Lake Hotel. Fy-Cross, Anglesey.

CONNEMARA.—Several thousand acres well preserved general shooting. Wildfowl shooting, lake and sea fishing good. All kinds of boats at hand. Terms moderate. Peter Conroy, Hotel, Kilkerrin, Connemara.

SHOOTING to let 300 acres. Apply T. Down, Hansford, Chumleigh, N. Devon.

Figure 11. Advertisement for outdoor workers in The Shooting Times and British Sportsman, 12 October, 1895.

flowers, fruit and vegetables being despatched to a high-class greengrocer and florist in Harrogate.

Not all gardeners were happy with these arrangements. Bob Gregory, who worked at Luton Hoo after the Second World War, noted that the kitchen gardens began to be run on a semi market garden basis. He had to go to Covent Garden once and then twice a week with the estate van loaded up with produce. When the head gardener was told that he must make up the wages of twenty-one men and boys out of the sale of garden produce, Gregory decided to leave. 'The business side of market gardening did not appeal to me at all', he wrote. So in 1948 he successfully applied for the position of head gardener at Bitham Hall, Warwickshire.[13]

Garden Staff

Gardeners were the most numerous of male outdoor servants during the nineteenth and early twentieth centuries. Their duties ranged from those of an odd-job man in a small household to the specialised skills of a Joseph Paxton, able to win medals and awards at horticultural shows, and having these successes reported in the gardening press. *The Gardeners' Chronicle* in particular, provided detailed career profiles of some of the leading gardeners of the day, as well as lengthy obituaries when they died. These are an invaluable source of information for genealogists whose ancestors happen to have been gardeners. They also reveal that a substantial proportion of the men were themselves the sons of gardeners or small farmers.

Typical of many was George Sage, who in 1875 was in charge of Earl Brownlow's kitchen garden at Ashridge Park near Tring. Sage was born in 1824, the son of a head gardener on a small estate at Hillingdon Heath. When he left school at thirteen he worked with his father for three years before moving to Uxbridge Common, where he stayed for five years. After that he worked for a banker at Uxbridge before moving to the prestigious Rothschild property, Gunnersbury Park. There he had 'good practice in the different departments', with pineapples, cucumbers and mushrooms among the specialities grown there. In 1849 he went to Chatsworth, where he remained four years, before obtaining a post as foreman gardener at Crystal Palace. From there he went to Ashridge in January 1858, on the strength of a recommendation from Joseph Paxton. Sage was also a successful exhibitor - something which was considered very important in enhancing a gardener's reputation and that of the property on which he worked. He noted proudly that he had 'taken the gold medal of the Royal Botanic Society'.[14]

12. A gardener and gardener's boy with a potato planter c.1900. (Centre for Oxfordshire Studies and Oxfordshire County Council Photographic Archive).

Some head gardeners were regular contributors to the gardening journals of the day, thereby adding to their income and their status. Ambitious men were expected to keep up with the latest literature and the most modern techniques of plant propagation and cultivation.

Gardening in large establishments of the kind in which George Sage worked involved the use of hothouses, greenhouses and conservatories to produce exotic fruit, vegetables and flowers. In the later Victorian period orchids seem to have exerted what Jane Brown has called an 'obsessional sway' among estate owners and their gardeners.[15] Luxuries such as strawberries, pineapples, melons and grapes were grown in season and out, while the kitchen garden fulfilled the essential role of producing vegetables for the table. Flowers were raised in profusion to decorate the house and to provide an impressive display for important occasions such as balls, large dinner parties and public meetings. Oswald Stokes, who worked for the Legh family at Lyme Park in the early twentieth century was responsible for floral decorations at the house. That included raising plants for the windows in the long Bright gallery. 'It used to take 400 plants to decorate those windows ... You had to get everything just perfect for Mrs. Legh'.[16] When the Leghs moved to London for the Season, produce had to be packed and sent by rail for use in the town house. Joseph Addison, the head gardener, carefully despatched grapes, peaches, nectarines, strawberries and flowers so that they arrived at their destination in prime condition.

Head gardeners were periodically required to re-model the properties on which they worked. Thomas Speed, who became head gardener at Chatsworth in 1868, had immediately before this been employed by Sir Edward Walker at Berry Hill in Nottinghamshire. Whilst there he had 'laid out the flower garden anew, replanted all the vineries, built a range of Pine-stoves, [that is, heating for the raising of pineapples], replanted all the Peaches' and carried out a general re-organisation.[17] Gardens and parks had also to be prepared for games such as archery, croquet, lawn tennis and cricket, as well as for family tea parties and children's play.

Some estate owners followed the example of the Duke of Somerset in drawing up a formal contract with their head gardener. An agreement between the Duke and John Prouse for the post of head working gardener at Bulstrode Park, Buckinghamshire, in January 1883 shows that Prouse was to be paid £65 per annum for the first year, rising to £70 in the second. Coal and wood were to be supplied for his use, 'according to the rate received by the late Gardener during his term of over 20 Years residence. No perquisites allowed; nor Ground permitted to be cultivated on his own account - but he will have the usual fair allowance of vegetables for his own consumption.' Prouse, who was then aged twenty-eight, had previously been employed in six different country house gardens over a period of twelve years before he entered the Duke's service. At his last position at Rufford Abbey in Nottinghamshire he had not only been responsible for the kitchen, fruit and flower gardens, but for any bouquets and button-holes required, as well as for floral decorations in the Abbey itself.[18]

Advertisements of vacancies in *The Gardeners' Chronicle* indicate what was expected of head gardeners and their underlings, and how these changed over time, as the prestige of head gardeners rose in the later Victorian period, and as the swelling ranks of estate owners and the *nouveaux riches* created an ever greater demand for their services. The skills required became more complex, too, as a result of the growing interest in cultivating unusual or exotic plants and fruit. Some of these were brought back to Britain by the increasing body of professional plant-hunters. Hence on 25 November 1882, there was an appeal from 'Hortus' in *The Gardeners' Chronicle* for 'an exceptionally good Working HEAD GARDENER, who understands the routine of a first-class establishment, ... including Hard-wooded plants and Orchids, and growth of Specimen Plants ... Scotchman preferred'. The advertiser noted that separate foremen were employed for the glasshouses and for the raising of fruit, although they would, of course, work under the head gardener.

A successful practitioner added lustre to an estate by making it a goal for visitors and an attractive setting for garden parties and other events. At Chatsworth, Robert Aughtie noted in his diary during the late 1840s the large number of parties who came to inspect the gardens and were shown round by him or one of his fellow workers. This could be a lucrative sideline where tips were forthcoming, but on 31 July 1848, Aughtie noted with disgust that after he had shown round a big party from Sheffield, they had given him 'only seven pence at which I was vexed.[19]

Much depended, however, on the attitude of the head gardener. William Cresswell, employed as second man in the large Audley End kitchen garden during July 1874 showed visitors around the garden on his own initiative because he could not find Mr. Bryan, the head gardener. Bryan took exception to this and relations between the two became strained. Eventually on 31 August 1874, following a general reorganisation, Cresswell was given a month's notice to leave. With some difficulty he found a post as head gardener on a far smaller property.[20]

At Chatsworth the undergardeners were exhorted to keep diaries, with comments recorded on new plants, weather conditions and daily activities. Encouragement was given to them to visit other gardens, to compare developments there with Chatsworth, and this was something that Robert Aughtie did from time to time.[21] Joseph Paxton insisted on 'prompt attendance, good order, and sobriety' among his subordinates and contravention of these rules could lead to dismissal. During the summer months working hours were from 6 am to 6 pm, with a half-hour for breakfast and an hour for lunch, but during the winter the hours varied according to the weather. Fines were levied, so that sixpence had to be paid for arriving later than ten minutes after the lodge bell had rung, and the substantial sum of two shillings was required from anyone absent without permission, even on Christmas Day. Sixpence had to be paid by any man 'found lounging or wasting time' or failing to clean and stack properly the tools allocated for his use.[22]

The prime duty of the kitchen gardener was to supply the vegetables needed for daily consumption. Jane Brown has labelled the walled kitchen garden 'the temple of garden labour' and *The Gardeners' Chronicle* too, stressed its importance. Produce was normally supplied after consultation between the cook and his or her employer, and some cooks summarily rejected vegetables that were not in perfect condition. At Stoke Bruerne in Northamptonshire in the 1930s Bob Gregory, as a young gardener, remembered that the vegetables had to be delivered each day to the house promptly at 9 am, loaded on a special two-wheeled handcart. If anything 'was soiled the head-cook would reject it'.[23] At Calke Abbey a special tunnel was constructed in the early nineteenth century so that the gardeners could approach the house without encountering members of the family or their guests who might be strolling in the pleasure grounds.

Long hours of trenching, potting-up, planting out, hoeing, and watering formed what has been called 'the basic drudgery' of a gardener's life.[24] It was customary for youths wishing to work on landed estates to go as apprentices for a few years before moving on to become journeymen and then foremen. During their training they might have to pay a fee to the head gardener, while they worked in the different departments. Bob Gregory considered that a minimum of two years was needed to understand the intricacies of the kitchen garden and at least three years for the pleasure grounds, including learning how to propagate plants. He thought the greenhouses were the most important part of the garden because of the special care needed to supply the appropriate heating, lighting and ventilation. He also remembered the strict discipline imposed at Stoke Bruerne by the head gardener, Mr. Valentine. Work began at 7 am and ended at 5 pm but there were no tea breaks or annual holidays. 'When it came to our turn to look after the greenhouses at the weekend, we had 10/- (50p) extra'. Every man had to go to work each day with a clean collar and well polished boots. During the winter, when leggings were worn, these, too, had to be polished. The hinges of gates and doors had to be kept well oiled, and every Saturday the potting-shed was scrubbed out. All garden tools were oiled and hung up in readiness for a weekly inspection by the squire, Captain Meade.

When young unmarried men started their training on an estate they were often housed in a bothy, or kind of hostel. According to Frank Copcutt, who worked at Cliveden between the wars:

> you wasn't a gardener in my day, unless you lived in a bothy ... Bothies ... was for single people, and that was, really, your training ... All these estates had a bothy for gardeners as well as grooms, and you went from one to the other to get your experience ... The bothy ... was maintained by the Astors, the furniture and the linen. And they... was responsible for your bed linen, and your heating and cleaning and cooking. All you had to do was buy the food ... We had vegetables given us mind you, [but] we didn't get milk at Cliveden ... some bothies gave you milk as well.[25]

The Astors had two bothies for the gardeners and one for the stable grooms. All were kept clean by housekeepers. The accommodation was cramped, with two men sharing a room, and there was a single communal sitting-cum-dining room. But conditions generally were reasonable. In earlier years that had not always been the case. Daniel Judd, who began gardening at Brockett Hall, home of Lord Melbourne, in the late 1820s, remembered the bothy he shared as 'a wretched place, situated between and joining two stokeholes, one miserable room at the back of the [glass] houses .. [The] roof [was] covered with old-fashioned pantiles, without any ceiling, so when there came a drifting snow it found its way to us as we lay in bed'. Nevertheless he remained there for between two and three years, before being appointed to the Royal kitchen garden at Kew.[26]

Many head gardeners had a strong sense of their own position, and that applied not merely to their dealings with subordinates but to their employers as well. In the 1930s Lady Hyde Parker at Melford Hall recalled the humourless head gardener there as having 'quite an air' about him, with his black trousers and jacket, bowler hat, and green baize apron. 'If I took a peach from a wall while passing through the garden on a summer's day, Pomfret knew at once, and ... he managed to convey... that he disapproved strongly'. In similar circumstances Charles Wade grumbled that at his family home at Yoxford in Suffolk the head gardener had 'become such an autocrat, it ceased to be our garden any more, it became his garden, in which we were allowed to walk'.[27]

The superior status enjoyed by skilled gardeners applied not merely on large estates but to the increasing number of men employed by middle-class families. There they worked alone, either on a full or a part-time basis, or they were recruited as jobbing gardeners and handymen. Katharine Hopkinson, the daughter of a leading Manchester businessman, remembered the gardener at her Alderley Edge home had a strongly proprietorial attitude towards the garden and its contents. Even her mother had to show much tact in persuading him that surplus flowers and vegetables should be donated to Manchester hospitals, or that fruit from the glasshouse that had been carefully nurtured by him might be given to friends: 'no premature baby could have been snuggled into its cotton-wool jacket more carefully than Grundy wrapped up ... his precious peaches and grapes'.

Only those at the bottom of the gardening hierarchy, without specialist training, were treated with scant respect. This is likely to have been the fate of the successful applicant who answered an advertisement in *The Field* of 14 August 1886, for a young groom. He was to weigh about 9 stone and be a good rider, but he had also to 'make himself generally useful, waiting at table when required', and to have charge of the greenhouse. It is unlikely that he would have brought much knowledge to this latter task. Similarly, Vanessa Bell had little time for Walter Higgens, the Sussex man who married her long-serving maid, Grace, in May 1934 and who became the gardener at Vanessa's home, Charleston. She referred to him as the 'Dolt' and in a letter to a friend, Jane Bussy, in June 1940 made clear her low opinion of him: 'I have driven the Dolt with such an iron rod all these months that we really have plenty of cabbages ... Poor man, I have no mercy on him'.[28]

Stable Workers

In Victorian Britain, as, indeed, in earlier centuries, the quality of a family's carriage, rather like a modern household's motor car, was seen as an indicator of their affluence and social standing. In the eighteenth century this had sometimes been carried to excess so that in 1777 the *Morning Post*, when commenting on Lord Derby's equipage, drew attention to the elaborate livery worn by the coachman and the attendant footmen, 'with their red feathers, and flame-coloured silk stockings'. This made them look like 'so many figurantes taken from behind the scenes of the Opera House'.[29] In the nineteenth century coachmen usually wore more sober livery than this, but their importance as symbols of their employer's position in the world remained. Samuel and Sarah Adams in *The Complete Servant* underlined this in 1825 when they declared that on the 'sobriety, steady conduct, and respectable appearance' of the head coachman, depended 'the exterior appearance of the family' whom he served:

Every genuine Coachman has his characteristic costume. His flaxen curls or wig, his low cocked hat, his plush breeches, and his benjamin surtout, his clothes being also well brushed, and the lace and buttons in a state of high polish. Care in driving his horses so as to preserve his own family and not injure other passengers on horse or foot ... is of the utmost consequence. It is his business to have the carriage kept in repair, and to prevent his master being imposed upon by wanton charges: and in like manner to advise and assist in the purchase of horses, and in this delicate business, protect the interest of his employer.

A competent man might also carry out simple repairs. In June 1849 John Farron, the single-handed coachman employed by Benjamin and Mary Anne Disraeli, received an additional 15s to supplement his quarterly wage of £6 5s to recompense him for 'cleaning and oiling the chariot' and carrying out some repairs to the barouche. [30] In many families coachmen were allowed to sell the old wheels of the coach as a perquisite, and there were allegations of unscrupulous men speeding the process along by boring holes in the spokes.[31]

A good coachman was expected to drive smoothly but not too swiftly. Mrs. Beeton suggested that a pace of seven or eight miles an hour should be aimed at, since 'less speed is injurious to the horses, getting them into lazy and sluggish habits'. He should rarely use the whip and when driving 'the coachman should never give way to temper'.[32]

Where two coachmen were kept and the stable establishment was large, *The Servants' Practical Guide* (1880) suggested that the head coachman would drive a pair of horses in the barouche or other open carriage, while the second coachman drove the one-horse brougham. He would also undertake any night work required, such as driving the family to a ball or a dinner, and carrying them to and from a railway station.

The stable staff usually began work at between 5 am and 6 am on what was a seven-days-a-week routine. The first hour and a half was spent mucking out the stables and dressing the horses. 'Washing and cleaning carriage and harness would take between two and three hours,' declared *The Servants' Practical Guide*, 'and the vehicle would be at the door by eleven o'clock, its windows open and the interior purged of all fustiness.' Instructions must be given beforehand as to which direction the horses were to face, since it was considered a sign of bad management if the carriage had to be turned in the street.

The coachman was assisted by grooms and, in large establishments, by stable boys, too. They were responsible for feeding and exercising the horses and, if necessary, acting as postilions and outriders. At Petworth there were twenty-four coachmen and grooms at work in the late Victorian period, while at Longleat around the same time fourteen men and boys were employed. They included a coachman, a second coachman, a carriage groom, a steel-boy, who burnished the bits and metal parts of the harness, and a 'tiger'. He was a small boy in livery who sat upright on the box of the carriage, with his arms folded across his chest, and whose role was primarily ornamental. However, he did have another responsibility, to lead the ponies of the younger children of the household should they go out riding. When the family moved to London for the Season they took eleven horses and five stablemen with them. At the rear of the Marquis of Bath's Grosvenor Square town house there were mews, with stables and a coach house, and above these were rooms for the coachmen and grooms to use as lodgings.[33]

When at home on the country estate the unmarried grooms usually lived over the stables and were allowed board wages or, as at Cliveden in the 1930s, they lived in a bothy. The married men normally had a cottage of their own.

Where the family went hunting, each person riding to hounds needed two horses. One of the grooms rode the spare horse, making sure it experienced as little stress as possible, so that it was relatively fresh when an exchange was effected later in the day. Alfred Tinsley, who went into 'gentlemen's service' in 1922, was one who carried out this task among his other duties. He remembered his master provided him with a smart new hunting outfit each year, consisting of a bowler hat, half-a-dozen hunting ties, dark jacket, lighter breeches, and plain hunting boots. 'The boss would have to see you were well turned out ...to keep his own credit up ... And the wages were good, too'.[34]

The grooms usually taught younger members of the family to ride. At Cliveden this responsibility was taken on by Brooks, the head groom. Michael Astor remembered him as a dapper man with a brisk manner. 'Riding was a serious form of pleasure; it was fun but it was not frivolous. Brookie ... took pride in his work, in his horses and, I think, in us. His job was simply to take us riding and he made it as interesting as he could'.[35] However, Michael's favourable opinion of Mr. Brooks was not shared by his staff. According to another of the Cliveden outdoor workers, he was a martinet:

> You used to get a medal if you'd been there for about six weeks ... They used to get a drink of tea and I've seen [the grooms] running back to work ... and every morning,

exercising and coming back, doing this - they used to be swilling down those cobble stones ... every morning and it could be freezing, and they was doing it, and they'd be throwing down sand after them ... They were all different every time you'd see them.[36]

Coachmen and grooms were expected to be of light weight, so as to avoid putting strain on the horses. Consequently advertisements inserted by, or for, stable staff often mentioned a candidate's weight. In The *Field* of 3 July 1886, a man who was seeking a situation as a coachman or groom and coachman, noted that he could 'ride and drive well; two years' excellent character; aged 30, height 5 ft. 5 ins., weight 9 st 10 lb; leaving through family going abroad'. In another case, Admiral Arthur Cumming of Foston Hall in Derbyshire, advertised for a post for his head groom; 'seven years' character for honesty and sobriety, during which he has had entire charge of a stud of hunters; light weight, rides well, and breaks horses'

.

Coachmen were often recruited from the ranks of experienced grooms and sometimes, as at Nuneham Courtenay, wages books show that there were in-house promotions. Thus in 1872, Joseph Smith was a groom at Nuneham, one of three men in the stable and earning £20 per annum. By 1878 he had become the second coachman at £32 per annum, while the stable staff had increased to four. Two years later he had become head coachman, at £40 a year. He was still in that position and earning the same rate of pay in 1898, when the wages book series ended. At that date the second coachman was Alfred Pitson, who received £20 a year. According to the 1891 population census, he, too, had worked as a groom. At Nuneham, the coachman was provided every year with two suits of livery; two stable suits; two hats; a pair of top boots; and 10s 'glove money'. He was to receive a new great coat every two years. The second man also had two suits of livery per annum but only one stable suit and one hat, while he was to receive top boots every two years, a great coat every three years, and gloves when required'.[37] So were the distinctions drawn.

In the late Victorian period, and more particularly in the early twentieth century, many well-to-do families started to purchase motor cars and consequently reduced their stable staff. In 1901 there were still 75,355 domestic coachmen and grooms recorded in the population census for England and Wales, but by 1911 that had fallen to 67,228. There was now a new category of domestic motor-car drivers and attendants, who in 1911 already numbered 23,151. After the First World War their number increased and in the view of Barry Skirrow, chauffeur at Castle Howard in 2000, the 'golden era of chauffeuring was from the 1920s to the 1950s'.[38] Sometimes, as at Lyme Park, a coachman might be sent for training to become a chauffeur. For in the early days motor cars needed a good deal of maintenance and that was one of the chauffeur's responsibilities. Many early chauffeurs were trained at the factories where the vehicles were manufactured. Certain grandees appointed French or German drivers, and that included the ninth Duke of Marlborough, who had a French chauffeur at Blenheim. In 1907 the Duke owned a Humber car and paid the chauffeur the substantial sum of £16 a month. His livery cost £8 2s 6d and he had an assistant to help clean, polish and maintain the ducal vehicles.[39]

The wider use of motor transport from the 1920s, coupled with financial pressures, meant that outdoor staff numbers were reduced. One or two chauffeurs could replace a dozen or more grooms and helpers. Wealthy families like the Astors had as many as five chauffeurs, each with his own particular role. That included one each for Lord and Lady Astor. Noel Wiseman, a former agent on the Cliveden estate, remembered that Lord Astor's chauffeur would not drive Lady Astor, or vice versa, because 'if he wasn't there on the doorstep when he [Lord Astor] wanted him, if somebody else had taken him ... there was trouble ... Then we had a horse-box driver, carted the horses about; two driver-mechanics who also included things like mower repairs when they'd got time.'[40]

Even in the heyday of the coachman and groom, the majority of stable staff worked in small establishments, where, as with the Disraelis' coachman in the 1840s and 1850s, they were either alone or aided by a young stable boy. In middle-class households a groom would be expected to look after the horses, ride out with messages, and be able to drive a pony carriage. But he might have to help around the house and garden, too, perhaps acting as a footman or waiter from time to time. On occasion these all-purpose servants lacked sufficient time to wash themselves properly before they waited at table, and the odour of the stables all too unpleasantly assailed the noses of the diners.

Gamekeepers and Foresters

Unlike gardeners and grooms, gamekeepers and foresters were employed on substantial landed estates only. Gamekeepers, in particular, were associated with the major country sports of shooting, fishing and deer stalking. The right to kill game was historically a closely guarded privilege based on property ownership and social position. From 1710 a landowner could appoint a gamekeeper authorised to kill game on the estate and whose name had to be recorded with the Clerk of the Peace which issued Gamekeepers' Certificates at a cost of one shilling. Registers of Gamekeepers' licences and Certificates to Kill Game can be found in Quarter Session Records in County Record Offices. See Jeremy Gibson's guide to *Quarter Session Records,* 1995 for lists of surviving licences.

It was during the second half of the nineteenth century that their number and importance increased rapidly, as shooting gained in popularity, encouraged by the enthusiasm of the Prince of Wales for the sport and by the money and interest of some of the *nouveaux riches* landowners who had accumulated their wealth in manufacturing or commerce before buying or renting an estate. One of the best known of them was Lord Iveagh, a member of the Guinness brewing family. He purchased the Elveden estate in Suffolk in 1894 and turned it into one of the premier shooting properties in the country. At Elveden there was a staff of around seventy full-time gamekeepers, under-keepers, wire-fencemen, and warreners, who dealt with the immense numbers of rabbits. By 1912-13 the head of game shot in a season had reached 77,723, including 24,619 pheasants and 3,532 partridges. This compared to the 24,731 head shot in 1894-95, of which 15,100 had been pheasants and 1,978 partridges.[41] Tom Turner, who became head keeper at Elveden, claimed it was shooting rather than farming that 'took priority over everything else on the estate.' Much the same applied to the royal estate at Sandringham, where on the day prior to a big shoot, an order was issued forbidding all work on the land 'for fear of disturbing the game.' On the day of a shoot there was a virtual curfew, with no machinery allowed to move and nobody permitted to go on the roads except those connected with the shoot.[42]

Interest in game preservation began to grow in the late eighteenth century, with an increasing demand for bigger 'bags' of game leading to the setting up of separate game departments on estates. The battue system was established whereby beaters drove the birds towards the guns, so that sportsmen no longer had to search out their quarry. The new trend was underlined by the fact that from 1785 a tax was levied on those killing game, with a special rate of 10s. 6d. (52½p) per head for gamekeepers who were employed as professional servants. For the first time this meant the total of keepers could be assessed, and in 1825 their number was put at 3,826. But other staff were needed, too, such as watchers to keep a look out for poachers. In the early nineteenth century Sir Robert Peel was said to employ five assistants for every keeper.[43]

In the Victorian era interest in the sport further intensified, helped by improvements in the guns used and by the construction of the railways, which made shooting estates more accessible. In these circumstances the number of gamekeepers grew rapidly, rising from 12,633 in 1881, according to the census of population for England and Wales, to 17,148 in 1911, although, as mentioned earlier, the census report itself considered this latter figure an underestimate.[44] In the major game preserving counties of Norfolk and Suffolk by 1911 there were three or four gamekeepers in every village, and in those two counties they outnumbered the police. The head keeper had a good deal of authority on an estate and his word was law. Often he was more respected, and feared, by villagers than the village policeman, especially where suspected poachers were concerned. As Norman Mursell, who became head keeper at Eaton in Cheshire, commented: 'The gamekeeper was always about and had to be very, very observant,' thereby providing security 'not just only for the game department but for the whole of the estate'.[45]

Shooting parties became major social events and there was increasing competition between estates as proprietors vied with one another to produce the best sport and the largest 'bags'. This meant great attention was paid to the rearing of pheasants, which formed the principal quarry. At Elveden by 1914 as many as twenty thousand of these were raised in a year and the way the policy was implemented can be illustrated from the Duke of Westminster's Eaton estate. There around the middle of the nineteenth century an average season's bag had been around 1,000 pheasants, and 500 partridges, plus hares, rabbits and woodcock. During the 1880s, the Duke began to rear more pheasants and by the 1890s bags had risen to between 5,000 and 6,000 birds in a season. On the eve of the First World War there were about twenty gamekeepers at work on the estate.

Much depended on the skills of the head gamekeeper and his staff if there were to be successful breeding. Their work involved collecting eggs from the laying hen pheasants, either in the wild or from a special laying ground, where hundreds of hen birds and a small number of cocks were brought together in the spring. In addition, specialist game farms offered eggs for sale to proprietors anxious to boost their stock. The eggs were hatched by broody hens, purchased from local farmers, rather than by the pheasants themselves. When the chicks hatched they were taken with the hens to coops already set up in a large rearing field, where they were fed and watered three or four times a day by the keepers. When the coops were all filled with chicks, each man on a large shooting estate might have as many as a hundred coops to attend to. Many hours were spent mixing the special feed and then walking round to distribute it. After about six weeks the young birds, now known as poults, were taken to the woods and released. For a time they were still fed by the keepers until they had become settled into their new location.

In addition to carrying out these tasks, however, a keeper had to look after his beat. That meant searching out wild partridge nests, destroying vermin such as rats, stoats, weasels and other predators that might threaten the game birds, and keeping a look out for poachers. Traps, poison and shooting were all used to kill predators and it was common for the heads and tails of stoats, weasels and rats to be nailed to a keeper's gibbet to demonstrate his diligence to his employer. In the opinion of

Tom Turner the destruction of vermin was a keeper's most important task and it was 'the duty of the Head Keeper to see that his under keepers [carried] this out'.[46]

The skills; expected from a gamekeeper were listed in advertisements inserted for, or by, workers in sporting journals like *The Field*, *The Shooting Times* and *The Gamekeeper* during the Victorian and Edwardian period. Typical of many was the appeal in *The Shooting Times* of 5 October, 1895, inserted by L. Moseley of East Marden in Sussex. He was seeking a situation as a single-handed or beat gamekeeper:

> thoroughly understands pheasant and partridge rearing and breaking young dogs, is a good ferreter and trapper, wirer of rabbits, and understands all duties of gamekeeper, or would take job rabbit catching; height 5 ft. 10 in.; weight, 12 stone; strong and active; excellent character.

The Gamekeeper, which was first published in 1897, also offered an employment register to keepers seeking a new post and to estate owners wanting staff. However, as in its issue of February 1900, it warned potential applicants against nurturing unrealistic expectations: 'Mere lads of 18 and upwards often state that they require head-places, with several men to assist, and ask exorbitant sums for their services, which they must know there is little chance of obtaining'. The journal also published career profiles of successful head keepers. As in the case of Mr. G. O. Potter, head gamekeeper at Aldermaston Park near Reading, these usually emphasised success in rearing large numbers of birds. At Aldermaston, the 'average bag is 5,000 pheasants, 300 partridges, 100 wild ducks and 2,000 rabbits.' Mr. Potter had five under-keepers regularly employed as well as a number of occasional helpers, and he also looked after a herd of about eighty roe deer.[47] Some head keepers even sent details of successful shoots to *The Gamekeeper*, presumably to broadcast their achievement and that of their staff. In November 1900, J. Hague, head keeper at Holwick Moor near Darlington reported that from August to October in that year a total bag of 3,170 brace of grouse had been recorded on the moor.

Nine months of the keeper's year were spent preparing for the shooting season, which began with grouse on the 'glorious Twelfth' of August. Many grouse moors were in Scotland or the North of England and English landowners either purchased or rented a Scottish shooting lodge so that they could participate in the sport and in fishing and deer stalking. According to Jonathan Ruffer, the head keepers in Scotland had a good deal of authority, being in charge not only of game shooting but also of fishing and deer stalking. Many, both there and south of the border, came into the occupation because their father or another close relative had been a gamekeeper, and from an early age they had started to learn the skills needed.

When a shoot was held it was customary on many estates to dress beaters and keepers in a distinctive livery. The beaters usually wore white smocks, sometimes with red collars, and with a red band on their hats. This had two purposes. First it prevented unauthorised people from joining in the shoot as beaters, and second it made them more visible when they were driving the game, and consequently less likely to be accidentally shot. Usually the beaters came from among the agricultural workers and woodmen on the estate, although additional men and boys might be brought in if needed. When Norman Mursell went as a trainee to Eaton in 1929 he recalled there were over eighty beaters, some of whom were used as 'stops' to prevent the pheasants from escaping into nearby hedgerows and fields during a drive. He also remembered the special livery worn by the Eaton keepers. This comprised a green velvet jacket and waistcoat, with white breeches, special leggings, and a hard bowler-type hat decorated with gold braid.[48] Norman himself had the humble role of cartridge carrier on this occasion and he and the other lads went out with the loader they were serving to the shooting stands. Once members of the shooting party had reached their respective pegs, the head keeper blew a whistle, and the beaters began work. A barrage of pheasants flew overhead, to provide targets for the waiting guns, while the loaders frantically inserted cartridges into the shotguns, so as to be able to keep the front man 'fed' with a loaded weapon.[49] When King George V shot at Sandringham he always employed one of the estate's agricultural workers as his loader, but some men brought along their butler or valet to carry out the task.

After each drive was completed the dead birds were picked up by specially designated men and their dogs. This included counting the numbers shot and allocating appropriate totals to each 'gun', before putting the birds into a game cart to be taken away to the larder. At Elveden, according to Tom Turner, a drive-by-drive record was quickly entered in a game book, and when the guns stopped for lunch a card showing the bag up to that time was handed in. But, as he drily admitted, 'handling such large numbers of game was an arduous job'. [50] Game books still survive for many landed estates, showing the number and kind of quarry shot and how it was disposed of. At Elveden, the great majority had to be taken from the hooks in the game larder, counted and packed for market early on the following morning, 'before the next day's bag of hot game began to arrive.'

As the gamekeeper's role grew in importance during the nineteenth century, he faced increasing hostility from other members of the rural community, who resented the powers he possessed to search labourers' cottages for snares, nets and illicit game, and who could haul poachers before local magistrates for summary trial and punishment. Fox hunters, too, were another group of opponents, suspecting the keepers of vulpicide in their relentless efforts to destroy vermin. Farmers blamed them for the losses caused to crops by the game and the deer on shooting estates. One Scottish farmer declared angrily in the early 1870s: 'I call a game keeper's work doing nothing; the principal part of his business is tormenting the tenants.'[51] Fairman Joseph Mann, a Norfolk tenant farmer agreed, claiming that gamekeepers were 'generally troublesome to farmers ... They break the fences down very much and are always prowling about'.[52]

Finally, and most dangerously, keepers faced the hostility of poachers. As T.B. Johnson, author of *The Gamekeeper's Directory* (1851 edn) pointed out: 'It requires at least a full share of courage to face the danger ... to grope the way in the dark, ... liable at every step to be knocked down, or perhaps assassinated.' The fact that as late as 1915, the penalty for night poaching was three months' imprisonment for a first offence and seven years for a third added to the likelihood that poachers would resist violently if they were discovered.[53] Tom Turner remembered that at Elveden as many as twenty keepers and night-watchers would go out at a time to combat the activities of the poachers:

> Altogether we spent scores of nights 'lying out', many of them in stinging frost, biting winds, or driving sleet. Often have I walked the weary miles to my lodgings, not to sleep, but to arrive in time to start the day's work, turning out for night-watching again at the end of the day. [54]

It was in these circumstances that *The Gamekeeper* pointed out the damage to a keeper's health as a result of night watching during the winter months, when he had to stand motionless in order to avoid alerting potential poachers. It advised the taking of 'a small flask of liquid refreshment' to ward off a chill.[55]

At the end of the nineteenth century the battles between keepers and poachers were less vicious than during the difficult early years of the nineteenth century when some gamekeepers had been murdered. Between 1833 and 1843 alone at least forty-two keepers were killed in skirmishes with poachers, and in twenty-five of the cases a verdict of wilful murder was returned. By the 1890s the battles were less lethal but considerable force continued to be used on both sides. In December 1893, when Tom Turner was involved in the capture of poachers he lost the top of his knuckles as he protected his head against blows from the cudgels the men were carrying. When these particular gang members were brought to court they were sentenced to between two and three months' imprisonment with hard labour. But the trial gave rise to much bitterness from the friends and relatives of the poachers towards Turner when he gave evidence in the case.

Both *The Gamekeeper* and *The Shooting Times* include accounts of battles in the 1890s between poachers and keepers. At Badworth in Yorkshire in January 1893 a local labourer was brought before Pontefract West Riding Court charged with game trespass and with threatening to shoot an underkeeper, John Bailey. In this case he got off relatively lightly, being fined 18s. (90p) for the trespass and bound over in the sum of £5 for the threats. He also had to pay 16s. (80p) costs.[56]

Estate records may yield details of the conditions of service of individual keepers, as well as their rates of pay. Thus in 1885 George Pye was appointed by the Benyon family of Englefield to be keeper on the Mortimer beat of their estate. It was noted that he had previously worked for a landowner at nearby Hurley, and that he was aged thirty-four and was married: 'has reared Pheasants; look after the Woods and Farms; keep down the Rabbits and send them to Englefield.' He was to be given the keep of two dogs and provided with a helper at 15s. a week. His own wage was to be 20s. a week, plus a free house.[57]

Game books may also show that keepers were often expected to shoot game or rabbits for their employer's household and even to send these away to London, when the family was residing at their town house. At Nuneham Courtenay in 1881, when the Harcourts were at Hastings, pheasants and rabbits were sent there, too. During this period arrangements were made to sell surplus game from Nuneham to local dealers, and sales valued at around £130 were achieved between October 1880 and April 1881. This, too, was something which the head gamekeeper had to arrange. Rabbits were also given from time to time to the 'sick and poor'.[58] The game book of the Mentmore Estate in Buckinghamshire similarly reveals the sale of pheasants, hares and rabbits to dealers, with 2s. 6d. (12½p) per head received for the pheasants and hares, and 1s. (5p.) for the rabbits, in the early twentieth century.[59] There, too, gifts of rabbits to local cottagers were recorded.

On many estates the forestry department was closely associated with the requirements of game preservation. This was shown by the arrangement at Lord Rothschild's Tring Park estate in Hertfordshire, where the head gamekeeper was *ex officio* the head forester. In that way the 'interests of sport and timber did not conflict', comments Jonathan Ruffer, with small thickets and larger areas of woodland planted with the needs of the game in mind. Equally, however, the zeal of keepers in curbing hare and rabbit numbers was important in preventing damage to newly planted saplings. At Chatsworth in the 1930s, where the main priority remained the rearing of game, the then Duchess of Devonshire wrote plaintively in a notebook: 'Someone must decide whether rabbits or trees are to be grown on this estate'.

Figure 13. An advertisement in The Shooting Times and British Sportsman, *12 January, 1895 suggesting to gamekeepers one way of tackling poaching problems.*

After the First World War, on many less affluent estates than Chatsworth, financial pressures caused landowners to cut back on game preservation. In some cases, shoots were leased or rented to syndicates, so that at Elveden the second Lord Iveagh rented about 5,000 acres to a syndicate of six or seven guns from 1932 until the outbreak of the Second World War. The shoots were organised by the Elveden head keeper, Tom Turner, with the syndicate shooting on thirteen or fourteen days each year. Elsewhere, as at Petworth, owners simply reduced the number of gamekeepers employed and increased the size of the individual beats. In these circumstances, the overall total of keepers employed declined. In 1911 there had been 17,148 recorded in England and Wales and 5,908 in Scotland. Twenty years later the respective totals were 10,706 for England and Wales and 4,050 for Scotland, according to the 1931 population census. From then onwards the downward trend continued, under the influence of the Second World War, the subsequent increase in costs and taxes, and the general decline of the landed interest. Brian Martin suggests that by the early 1990s there were 'a mere three or four thousand keepers in full-time employment'. [60] It was a complete transformation from the situation a century earlier during the 'golden age' of the sporting estate.

CHAPTER FOUR
Hiring, Firing and Moving on

Getting a Place and Keeping It

U p to the mid-nineteenth century a majority of the population still lived in rural areas. Then, as industry and commerce expanded and employment on the land declined, there was a good deal of outward migration from many country districts. By 1901 nearly four-fifths of the people of England and Wales lived in urban communities compared to around a half who had been so located fifty years before. The change affected servant recruitment in that for much of the Victorian period something like two-thirds of male and female domestics were born in the countryside and then worked in towns. Not only were household posts limited in rural areas but for better-paid or more specialised positions the main openings were in urban areas. By 1901 just a quarter of the nation's domestic staff worked in country districts, according to the census returns.[1]

When a large part of the population still lived in villages or market towns the daughters of agricultural labourers, small farmers and craftsmen were available to meet the demand for servants. As their numbers dwindled towards the end of the Victorian period there were ever louder complaints

of servant shortage. To add to the problem, female employment outlets in factories, shops, the dress trades and even teaching were widening, with younger girls especially reluctant to accept the restrictions and the status ambiguities associated with servant life. Between 1881 and 1901, partly because of the raising of the minimum school leaving age, the proportion of female servants under fifteen years of age dropped by 34 per cent, and of those aged fifteen to nineteen by 7.3 per cent, while for women between twenty-five and forty-four they increased by 33.1 per cent. The domestic labour force was getting older and hence expected to command higher rates of pay.[2]

Mistresses preferred country girls because they were thought to be more honest, hardworking and biddable, as well as cheaper, than their urban counterparts. They were also considered more reliable in that if they lost their place or decided to leave on a whim, it was difficult for them to return home when their family lived a distance away. Charles Booth, in discussing the 'lower classes' of London-based servants during the 1890s commented on their 'very independent spirit' and the way in which even if they had agreed with a mistress to take a post, they 'not unfrequently [failed] to appear on the specified day. They [had] changed their mind, thinking the work too hard, or the neighbourhood too far away from their friends'. Another unsatisfactory aspect was 'the frequency with which girls [ran] away from their places instead of giving notice to leave', apparently because of 'a feeling of alarm at the formality of giving notice'.[3] Country girls were less likely to behave in this way, it was thought.

Another factor encouraging non-local recruitment was employers' desire for privacy. Often they did not want servants from the neighbourhood, especially in small households, in case they gossiped about the family to friends and relatives, or had hangers-on who visited the house clandestinely. Marion Sambourne, after a long search for a cook early in 1885 finally made an appointment, only to note a fortnight later: 'The cook [is] to depart at the end of the month untrustworthy, talks to the housemaid who is also going'. Presumably they were discussing the Sambournes.[4] This reticence even applied to mistresses of large country houses, at least as regards 'front of house' staff, such as butlers, footmen, housekeepers, parlourmaids and senior housemaids. Mrs. Kennard of Crawley Court, Hampshire in the late Victorian period was one who had a firm policy of taking servants 'from elsewhere rather than from Crawley itself'.[5]

According to Mrs. Beeton's *Book of Household Management* (1861), engaging domestic staff was 'one of those duties in which the judgment of the mistress' had to be 'keenly exercised'. To this end a personal interview with a potential maid was

NURSEMAID WANTED. Must be used to and fond of Children. Wages £10 to £12.—Mrs. TURNER, Kingsbury, Aylesbury.

WANTED, A GOOD GENERAL SERVANT age 25 to 30.—Mrs. WALTER PEARKES, 28 St. Albans Road, Watford.

WANTED, GOOD COOKS, GENERAL SERVANTS, and NURSE GIRLS.—Mrs. HEARN, Servants Registry, 1, Cambridge Street.

WANTED, at a small Private School, A GOOD STRONG GENERAL SERVANT, age from 18 to 20. Wages £12. Housemaid and boy kept.—Apply CHILTERN HOUSE, Wycombe.

Figure 14. Advertising for servants was one way of recruiting new staff. (Buckinghamshire Advertiser and Aylesbury News, 15 August, 1891).

desirable so as to assess her suitability. And in obtaining a character reference from a previous employer a personal visit was to be recommended, if at all possible. 'By this means', wrote Mrs. Beeton, 'you will be assisted in your decision of the suitableness of the servant for your place, from the appearance of the lady and the state of her house. Negligence and want of cleanliness in her and her household generally, will naturally lead you to the conclusion, that her servant has suffered from the influence of the bad example'. [6] However, as Marion Sambourne discovered, checking up on servants in this way could be very time-consuming. 'Went after cook's character' or 'Go at 2 after character of cook' are just two of many diary entries between 1883 and 1885.[7]

In seeking to fill domestic posts both mistresses and workers often relied on personal contacts and recommendations, perhaps passed on by friends or, in the case of servants, by relatives already in service. Sometimes applicants learned of a vacancy through local gossip or servant networks. A fourteen-year old Norwich girl remembered following a neighbour's daughter into a Beckenham household: 'she sort of recommended me'. In this case the mistress supplied the youngster's uniform, rather than expecting her to provide it for herself, as was customary. But it had to be paid for on an instalment system, at so much a month, when she began work. Like many young people in their first place, this girl found the transition from home life to work as a maid in a strange house a traumatic experience. She was very homesick and pleaded with her mother to be allowed to return: 'I wouldn't mind what I done when I come home if she only let me go home'. She wrote back and said, 'Be thankful you've got a bed to lie on and a good meal'. The girl added sadly: 'I didn't ask again'.[8] Out of her meagre wage of 8s. (40p) a month she sent 2s. 6d. (12½p) home.

Servant contacts, informing fellow workers of vacancies, were valued by those higher up the domestic scale, too. Frederick John Gorst learnt of an opening for a Royal footman at the Duke of Portland's Welbeck Abbey through a friend and fellow footman, who was also applying for one of the two posts on offer. [9] Both men were subsequently successful. But households where the mistress or the senior servants were hard to please might, by the same token, have difficulty in filling posts once the word got around. William Lanceley, whilst working as a house steward, remembered telling fellow servants when vacancies arose elsewhere, only to receive the reply: 'I don't think I should care to go there'. Earlier in his career he recalled two very large establishments 'which were always shunned by servants, and both were continually changing' because in one case the mistress was difficult and in the other the culprit was the house steward.

Figure 15. Girls at a domestic servants' training school conducted at Headington Hill Hall, Oxford, 1913 (Centre for Oxfordshire Studies and Oxfordshire County Council Photographic Archive).

Occasionally employers who moved away from their home area might seek to recruit a maid from their old community. Jane Welsh Carlyle appointed several servants from her native Scotland. This did not always prove successful. One long-serving Scottish maid had eventually to be dismissed because of persistent drunkenness and another, named Isabella, left within days, declaring 'no woman living could do the work' that the Carlyles expected from her.[10] However, fear of getting a bad character reference usually prevented discontented servants from being as outspoken as that.

Where personal recommendations failed, another possibility was to seek help and advice from local gentry or clergy in the villages, and from tradespeople in towns. Anne Sturges-Bourne, whose father was a Hampshire landowner and M.P., was one country house lady who regularly approached friends on behalf of her protegées, and was in turn contacted by them. In August 1850, she appealed to her close friend, Marianne Dyson, to look out for 'a place for a very nice girl of 15 whose father has been keeper/carpenter &c. a long time here, but he is an idle unsatisfactory servant, & I felt it right to part with him but shd. like to save his children ... This girl... is very clever ... She wd. like to be under a Lady's maid'.[11] Some parents, however, were not willing to let their daughter accept a post that Anne had found, either because they thought the girl was not robust enough or because they hoped she would go on to better things. On one such occasion, Anne noted that a Mrs. Callen would not 'let Mary go' to a place that had been located for her, on the 'plea of keeping her at home till her health is right, lest she shd. not be strong enough for nursery work'. Such rebuffs in no way dampened Miss Sturges-Bourne's enthusiasm, for as she confided to her friend in 1853: 'getting places and people to fit is one of the chief employments of life'. The use of tradespeople as employment agencies was a method recommended by Mrs. Beeton, when she pointed out that they were usually aware of 'those in their neighbourhood, who are wanting situations, and will communicate with them'. In Chelsea, Jane Carlyle found that one way of getting a maid was to inquire at the baker's shop.

A few girls left their home area and went to stay with friends or relatives who had already migrated, in order to seek a post. That was true of Nancy Jackman, a farmer's daughter from Devon. She went to London in 1854, when she was about sixteen, to stay with her brother, who was a saddler in Soho. With him she went to see a Mrs. Littler, who ran a grocer's shop in South Audley Street, to ask if she knew of a suitable vacancy. Mrs. Littler, 'liking the appearance of [Nancy] then fresh from the country', decided to engage her for her own household.[12]

Ambitious servants, especially those seeking lifetime employment in prestigious households, knew that during their youth they must move from place to place so as to gain experience and promotion. As Ernest King, who began his career as a hall-boy in a Devon landed family, recalled: 'I do not think it took me very long to grasp the fact that a man-servant, to learn his business must move from job to job ... It was necessary, however, to remain in each place for at least two years in order to obtain that precious passport - a reference. Houseboys and footmen, we fellows were just two a penny then, so that without a two-year reference no one would take you'.[13]

In country districts in the early Victorian years there was the possibility of attending an annual hiring or 'Mop' fair. But 'Mops' were increasingly criticised because of the rowdiness associated with them, as men and women stood around waiting to be hired. The Romany and Traveller Family History Society has published *A calendar of fairs & markets held in the 19th century* by Pat Loveridge, 2003 which is available at the Society of Genealogists library. By the final quarter of the nineteenth century, the fairs had fallen into disfavour except in the North of England and Scotland, where they were used mainly by farm servants. These were hired for six months or a year at a time. Marian Atkinson was only fourteen when she went to her first hiring fair at Ulverston in 1919. The servants lined up on one side of the street, and the farmers walked along looking 'you up and down'. They cross-questioned the girls as to what they could do and what pay they wanted. In the end, Marian recalled, a bargain was struck with one of them: 'he would lift his hand up, spit on it, and ... put his hand against mine. Then I got the [hiring] shilling ... I couldn't back out then'. Once she had got a place Marian rushed off with her friends to enjoy the fun in the fairground. 'The hiring was usually over by one o'clock'.[14]

An increasingly popular method of bringing together mistresses and servants was through advertisements in newspapers or specialist journals like *The Gardeners' Chronicle* or *The Shooting Times*. The use of advertising became more common as literacy standards rose and through the use of an accommodation address, perhaps that of the newspaper itself, a mistress could appeal for a domestic without revealing her identity. Prospective candidates could then be vetted before any were called for interview. Conditions could also be imposed, such as 'no Irish need apply' or the need for applicants to be of a particular age or religious denomination. After an unfortunate experience with an 'old half dead cook' in December 1846, Jane Carlyle inserted an advertisement in *The Times*. This produced a number of 'horrid looking females "inquiring after the place",' and one 'cheery little button of a creature' called Anne, whom she appointed. It proved a success and Anne was allowed to have a 'follower - the butcher's boy - in the kitchen for two hours a week. After nearly two years Anne married and left. But Jane had very variable relationships with her servants. Another Ann, appointed in May 1851, was initially praised as 'the best *character* I ever had in the house ... I hope she will stay – forever'. Unfortunately she had to leave for a short time on account of illness, but then returned in August 1853 and remained for nearly five years. However, by February 1858 she was being denounced as 'that unblessed' Ann, 'cunning, untrue, and intensely selfish'. When she gave notice and left in March 1858 her departure was greeted with relief.[15]

In the early twentieth century *The Times* encouraged servants to use its advertisement columns by arguing in 1907 that it was to their advantage to take a situation with employers who purchased an expensive newspaper: 'A family which pays 3d. for a daily paper (which is the price of *The Times*) instead of 1d. or ½d. is evidently a family of the best class, keeping a number of servants, so that they are company for each other. These families are just the people to offer a comfortable & permanent situation, & to appreciate good service ... They are not cheap, commonplace people'.[16]

The Lady magazine, too, after its launch in the mid-1880s concentrated on advertising servant vacancies among the social elite and offered 'Recommended Servants seeking places whose Mistresses will vouch for their character and capabilities'. Among those included were girls of a 'superior' social class, who were classed as 'ladies' who had fallen on hard times. Some preferred the title of 'Mother's Help' or 'Useful Help', to distinguish them from run-of-the-mill domestics. One such appeal inserted in *The Lady* was from a mistress living in Chiswick. She offered a good home 'to thoroughly domesticated MOTHER'S HELP. Not over thirty. Charge of two children. Must be a clever needlewoman. Servant kept'.[17] Not surprisingly, these 'lady servants' were not popular with their fellows below stairs on account of the airs many of them assumed and their unwillingness to take on the heavier domestic tasks. But their numbers in practice remained very small.[18]

Even the population-hungry colonies advertised for maids, offering free or reduced passages to those prepared to go overseas, particularly from the 1870s. In this case, however, the ulterior motive was probably a desire to obtain future wives for the predominantly male settlers rather than a wish to recruit mere domestic workers. Nonetheless rates of pay were undoubtedly better overseas than in England and Wales. At the end of the 1870s, fourteen year-old maids in New Zealand could earn 8s. a week, or more than twice what they would obtain in England. In January 1885, the proprietor of a recruitment agency in Auckland claimed that he had on his books more than fifty vacancies for all classes of servants. 'How easy it is girls for you to better your condition,' he declared. He pointed out that whereas in Britain general servants in their mid-twenties were receiving £10 a year, 'I positively should be in danger of my life were I to offer an Auckland General *that* wage, and a good wigging if I even offered double'.[19] Some women undoubtedly did respond to these appeals, but their total was limited.

When these alternatives failed, there were servant registry offices to contact. They increased sharply in the second half of the nineteenth century and were set up as specialist commercial organisations by some firms or as sidelines by people running other businesses. In Bulmer & Co.'s *History of Derbyshire*, published in the mid-1890s and including a detailed trade directory, fourteen registry offices were advertised in Derby itself. Of these, three were also dressmakers, two ran hosiery shops, and the rest included drapers, a general shopkeeper, a brush dealer and a stationery and newspaper vendor. Only four had no other occupation. But alongside these relatively small provincial agencies were prestigious London organisations like Mrs. Hunt's in Marylebone. There servant girls newly arrived in the capital in the late nineteenth century were offered sleeping accommodation on the premises while they waited to be hired. 'Fashionable ladies', it was said, 'had their own private cubicle, ... where they were in the habit of interviewing as many as twenty or thirty girls before deciding on one'.[20] For menfolk seeking superior positions as butlers or footmen in grand households there was 'Piercey's'. This was run by two former butlers and was used regularly by Arthur Richard Inch among others. Through it he obtained posts as first footman to the Duke of Marlborough at Blenheim Palace and later to the Marquess of Londonderry at his various mansions. This was during the 1930s but similar high quality registry offices existed in the Victorian years, too.

Philanthropic organisations, like the Girls' Friendly Society and the Metropolitan Association for Befriending Young Servants also had registry offices alongside their main preoccupation with providing leisure pursuits, moral guidance, and servant refuges for members who had lost their place or were too ill to work. By the 1880s the Metropolitan Association alone was placing about five thousand girls a year in the capital through its registry, though at a time when there were over a quarter of a million female domestics in London, its contribution was clearly modest.[21] In 1915, the newly-established Domestic Servants' Insurance Society, which offered sickness benefits, a convalescent home, and free dentistry to members, also set up an employment bureau. However, its role remained tiny. In the spring of 1915 the Society claimed a membership of 75,000 but during the six months June to December 1915 filled only 167 servant vacancies through its bureau.[22] Women seeking domestic places obviously preferred better-known agencies.

Even the new department stores began to provide servant employment bureaux. In 1895 Harrod's catalogue included an advertisement of its household services: 'Ladies will find this an excellent Medium for obtaining Companions, Governesses, Lady Helps, and all classes of Male and Female Domestic Servants ... No Registration Fee, but a charge of 5s. is made when suited. There is also a Special List of highly-recommended Cooks, Parlourmaids and Charwomen for Temporary Places or Dinner Parties, on Special Terms'.

However, some unscrupulous proprietors were accused of being more concerned to extract registration fees from employers and servants than with supplying appropriate domestic services. The controversial role some of them played during the depression years of the 1920s and 1930s is discussed in the next section, when surviving records for a few of the girls they recruited are also examined.

For mistresses seeking the cheapest maids, application could be made to workhouses, poor law schools, orphanages, correctional institutions like reformatories, and charitable bodies like the Foundling Hospital in London. The latter's extensive archives include employment registration books for apprentices as well as committee minutes, records of service and correspondence. They provide a fruitful source of information for those seeking to trace relatives who embarked upon their domestic career through this organisation. Small cash rewards were also offered to successful servants at the annual spring get-together held at the Hospital for the apprentices. At the end of an apprenticeship, those with good reports could earn a gratuity of up to five guineas [£5.25p]. This was normally received when they reached the age of twenty or twenty-one. Comments by masters and mistresses during the apprenticeship drew attention to their strengths and weaknesses and these can be supplemented by entries in the Secretary's letter books and in the Hospital's general committee minutes, when individual apprentices or employers are mentioned. A careful vetting of potential employers was carried out before the apprenticeship indentures were drawn up. Successful masters and mistresses had to be housekeepers, of the Protestant religion, must not let lodgings and, in the case of a male employer, they had to be married. The standard of accommodation offered was also considered, and during the apprenticeship regular reports regarding the conduct and diligence of the youngster were submitted. Some girls were very successful, like Jane Franklin, whose master and mistress in the spring of 1853 declared themselves 'well satisfied' with her 'in every respect'.[23]

But a number of apprentices were condemned as ill-tempered, disobedient and inefficient. Brought up in the institutional atmosphere of the Hospital they were unfamiliar with the routine of ordinary domestic life. Some were clearly overworked and received little sympathy from either their mistress or their fellow servants. An anonymous account of life as a domestic apprentice during the 1880s was published in 1919. It was probably written by Hannah Sherman, who was apprenticed to William Hicks, a diamond merchant, who lived at Hornsey. Although engaged ostensibly to help in the nursery, she spent fifteen hours a day on her feet carrying out all the dirty household jobs that the other servants did not want to undertake. 'Instead of being partly house and partly nursemaid, I was kitchen-maid, coal-porter, and messenger too. I was not fifteen, yet was worked like a cart-horse'. Her tasks included cleaning the family's boots in the cellar and washing her fellow servants' dirty clothes. 'In my endeavours to clean the articles I would always rub the skin off my fingers ... and would be soaked through to the skin before the evening'. [24] She wept many bitter tears at being treated contemptuously as a mere charity brat by the other members of staff. She was then accused of behaving impudently towards them, or of 'sullen behaviour towards the nurse'. Her master and mistress were quite kind but the problems with her fellow servants led to her being reassigned to other families on three separate occasions. Only in her fourth and last place, where she was the sole servant, were working conditions more congenial.

Another unfortunate foundling was Matilda Burney, who from an early stage in her apprenticeship to a Hampshire clergyman and his wife, in December 1852, was subjected to criticism and fault-finding. After about two years she was passed to the clergyman's mother but when she had been there around six months the complaints of ill-temper and unco-operative behaviour were revived. In February 1856 she was reassigned to Edward Bateman and his wife, in Islington, but a few months after that Mrs. Bateman wrote to the Hospital, claiming that Matilda was 'out of control' and would only do what she had a mind to do. In July 1856 she was returned to the Hospital and in May 1857 was allowed to emigrate to Australia, after being provided with an outfit by the Hospital. Yet, against this picture of persistent ill-temper and defiance towards her employers, must be set the letters she wrote while in service indicating her own deep unhappiness and loneliness. In 1854, for example, she wrote to her 'dearest Governess', probably Miss Soley, principal of the Hospital's girls' school, pleading with her to write and give her 'encouragement' and not to be 'angray' with her, because she was doing her best. But 'one word ... will be as bad as if I had don the world of evil things, dearest governess, will you healp me against this, your tender words will bring my high spirit down'. Later, when she was working for the Batemans, she asked the Hospital Secretary to allow her to have some of the cash that had been saved for her while she was a pupil, so that she could buy clothes, as her current pay of £6 a year was 'bearly enough' to keep her respectably clad. She also complained of having a bad neck and noted that some treatment she had received earlier had had to be ended because she could not afford to pay for it. 'When I am rich enough I shall go on with the treatment'.[25] Perhaps in Australia this deeply troubled girl was able to find some happiness and to have improved health.

Girls recruited from poor law institutions or from reformatory and industrial schools were other possibilities for mistresses seeking inexpensive servants or perhaps who were imbued with a charitable desire to give them a fresh start in life. . The Society of Genealogists' Library contains within its collections examples of apprenticeships from Lambeth Orphans Asylum showing girls as young as eight years old apprenticed in the "art of housewifery". Local parish records may well show similar apprenticeships for poor children.

In the case of those recruited from London poor law schools, from the mid-1870s their welfare when in service was under the supervision of the Metropolitan Association for Befriending Young Servants (MABYS). Some of their reports on the girls and their employers still survive so that in 1907, there are accounts of girls from the Kensington Union Schools at Banstead. One concerned Lily Matthews, aged sixteen, who was described as 'A good sensible girl doing well in her first place'. That was at Wallington. Those who proved incompetent or very inexperienced when they first went out, or who behaved badly might be passed on to a servants' training school. In 1907 this happened to fifteen-year-old Elizabeth Bushnell, who had been sent to a training home in Newbury, Berkshire and was reported 'so far' to have done well.[26] Elsewhere, for example in the case of pupils from the Central London School District, records of service survive and are indexed by name. They detail the name and address of the master or mistress of the girl, the size of the family she was serving, the nature of her duties, the kind of sleeping accommodation available, and whether there were other servants or not.[27] The records of London poor law unions, schools and institutions are to be published and indexed by Ancestry.co.uk

Poor law union minute books can also throw light on the fate of individual youngsters. On occasion girls might be sent to employers living a long distance away. In December 1876 Mrs. Perrin of Southport applied to Bicester workhouse in Oxfordshire for a maid and was sent twelve-year-old Maria Smith. Eighteen months earlier she had recruited another Bicester union servant, and the workhouse master had escorted her to Bletchley railway station to start her on her journey. As with the Foundling Hospital apprentices, not all of these arrangements turned out well. In January 1876 Mrs. Bond of Birmingham reported that Agnes Donavan, whom she had obtained from Bicester, had so badly 'misconducted herself' that she was unable to keep her, and she asked the poor law guardians to 'send some one to

Birmingham for her'. The workhouse master was given the task and duly brought Agnes back to the workhouse.[28] Mrs. Allnutt of London similarly complained that Louisa Brown, recruited from Bicester some time before, had recently become so 'untruthful and reckless that she could no longer keep her'.

But these adolescents, without friends or family, were always vulnerable to harsh treatment by employers or fellow servants. The fact that, like the Foundling Hospital girls, their only experience of domestic life before they went out was in helping to clean the institution where they resided meant they had little idea of what was involved in running a house. In 1874 an official report on the training provided for girls educated in 'pauper schools' called for better preparation to be made before they were sent out. Reports on individual youngsters noted that although they could carry out laundry-work and 'common scrubbing' - tasks they had performed in the workhouse or in a poor law school - they knew little of more intricate domestic tasks and were unable to cook. One girl claimed she had never been taught to light a fire or clean a grate but, declared her mistress, 'as she never spoke the truth about anything, probably she lied there'.[29]

Even at the end of the nineteenth century there had been few improvements. Most girls were still trained within the different departments of their own institution. Yet, in the 1890s, so acute was the demand for young and inexpensive maids that the opportunities for their employment were said to be 'practically unlimited'. For this reason the North Surrey District School at Anerley was able to insist that none of its girls was sent out as a single handed maid-of-all-work but was only to go where a second servant was kept, and where the starting pay was fixed at £6 per annum.[30] That was well above the £2 to £3 per annum secured by young poor law servants in earlier decades. Similarly in 1900 Norwich poor law guardians reported that 'the committee were quite crazed with applications from people who wanted ... servants', according to a report in the *Norfolk News* of 17 February in that year.

Sometimes institutions earned extra cash by running commercial laundries on the premises or by sending young inmates out as day servants. At the Mount Vernon Green reformatory school in Liverpool in 1890 a government inspector commented drily that the young laundry workers needed 'more outdoor exercise, and not quite so much devotion to the washing tub'. As well as taking in laundry from private families, nursing homes and some hotels, the school washed for the 150 boys on board a training ship moored in the area. It was heavy work, with the laundry floor constantly awash, and the dirty laundry arriving in giant skips. However, other domestic training, including cookery lessons, was given at Mount Vernon Green and in 1903 the school committee boasted that there was 'no difficulty in finding employment for our girls, as they are much sought after as servants. Some of them are getting £12 a year in their first place'.[31]

Girls from charitable and poor law schools or from corrective institutions like reformatories and industrial schools, normally had their first place found for them and, as with Foundling Hospital apprentices, could often only move to another post in their early days with the permission and support of the institution from which they came. Most servants, however, moved around of their own volition, in search of a better post or more congenial employers or fellow servants, or simply because they wanted a change. Some lost their place through illness, as Charles Cooper did when he caught scarlet fever while employed as a second footman by the Hankey family. 'I was very sorry when I heard that they had been obliged to fill my place, but one could hardly expect otherwise; in an establishment of that size, it was necessary... When fit to travel I returned to my home in London; not feeling very strong I rested for another fortnight before seeking another place'.[32]

Elsewhere the death of a master or mistress, or the break-up of a household for financial reasons might lead to dismissal. When Louise Creighton's parents ran into monetary problems in 1876, she advised her mother to dismiss all their existing servants 'who have been accustomed to a better state of things, & keep only three maid servants ... The outside I would keep only one regular gardener & a boy of 17 or so who would clean boots and knives, carry coal and milk cows and then help the gardener; he would cost less than a man'. The existing gardener should lose his job and be told that 'as you only meant to keep one you must have a young man who could work harder'.[33]

In large households senior staff hired and fired their subordinates. At Wilton between the wars, a daughter of the fifteenth Earl of Pembroke recalled their large retinue of retainers, including 'an absolutely marvellous butler ... Everything was done impeccably. If he felt somebody was really unsatisfactory, he would come and say, "I'm afraid George is no good. I think you'd better get rid of him," and he would then find somebody else. And the same for the housekeeper and cook.'[34] In these circumstances junior staff often regarded their seniors with a mixture of suspicion and apprehension.

In other cases servants were dismissed for various misdoings and misdemeanours, ranging from theft to insolence. Benjamin and Mary Anne Disraeli seem to have been particularly unfortunate with their male staff. In a relatively modest household of five or six indoor domestics, of whom two were normally men, between January 1845 to July 1852 alone they had eleven different under-butlers. One was dismissed for impertinence and another was sent away after less than three months as 'a great scamp, left the house for days at a time during our absence', presumably when he was acting in a caretaking capacity. A third man, Henry Newby, although he remained with the Disraelis for two years was criticised for being too dilatory when sent out with messages and when he was told to keep the urn clean, he sent it up a second time in the same dirty condition, much to his mistress's annoyance. During these seven and a half years there were also nine different footmen. One was too ill to take up his post and another left to go on the railway or join the police. Of the rest, one was discharged for drunkenness, two for impertinence, and one had part of his final wage deducted because he left behind a pair of old trousers instead of the new ones supplied as part of his livery. There was a rapid turnover of cooks and lady's maids, too, during these years, but only one housemaid. She remained until she eventually married from the house in May 1853. On that occasion the Disraelis supplemented her final pay with an extra pound as a wedding present.[35]

Some servants moved to another post as a way of showing their independence or in a spirit of defiance. That was true of a kitchenmaid employed at Haines Hill, Twyford in Berkshire. In July 1898 she wrote to a former colleague at Throckeevan, Hungerford, expressing satisfaction with her new place: 'I can swim in beer if I wish ... plenty kicking about. I wish you were here ... It seems a treat to be away from Throckeevan. Mrs. Wilton [the cook-housekeeper at Throckeevan] would have a fit if she had a fire going like we do. I put three scuttles of coal at once ... I never let on about the grub we had there to these servants. I would not let them know I was in such a show'.[36]

But whilst they were in a post fear of a bad reference kept most servants outwardly deferential, whatever their private thoughts about their employers and fellow staff members might be. If they found a place intolerable they made an excuse to leave, perhaps saying they had to return home to nurse a sick mother or that they were themselves too unwell to continue.[37]

Registry Offices

Servant registry offices had existed in the eighteenth century although then they often had an unenviable reputation as the resort of prostitutes and of the most incompetent workers only. Even in 1861 Mrs. Beeton had reservations, writing that whilst there were 'some respectable registry-offices, where good servants may sometimes be hired', the plan 'rather to be recommended' was for a mistress to make personal enquiries among acquaintances and tradesmen.[38] Nevertheless, during the second half of the nineteenth century their numbers increased rapidly and there were some, like Mrs. Hunt's in London or Massey's in Derby which counted members of the aristocracy and gentry among their clientele. According to the 1899 *London Post Office Trade Directory*, Mrs. Hunt's was the 'largest agency ever established', with a permanent staff of seventy-three people; 'letters in and out exceed 2,300 a day, an average of 155 persons being suited every day.' The business had existed for half a century and no fee was charged to either mistress or servant until the servant had taken up the place.

Charitable organisations, like the MABYS and the Girls' Friendly Society also helped to improve the reputation of registry offices. In 1890 the Girls' Friendly Society claimed to have received 10,927 applications from mistresses in the year as well as 7,741 from domestic workers seeking a place. However, its ability to match the two was less successful, with only 3,531 servants actually appointed.[39]

Hannah Cullwick made use of one of the respectable agencies at the Soho Bazaar, London, early in 1867. After she arrived she sat in the office with several other servants, waiting to have her name entered in the register.

> They have prayers there together at a certain time in the morning, and the man over it all wears a white tie, and speaks to us each about religion & gives us tracts before going up stairs to sit in the room where the ladies come to look at us ... I paid ½ a crown [12½p] - the price for the lower servants - it's 5/- [25p] for cooks or upper ones & I was shown ... where to wait ... the ladies begun to come in & I felt very nervous till one lady spoke to me & she ask'd me to follow her, & that was to another room where the ladies sat and hir'd you or ask'd you questions.[40]

If no engagement was secured on the first visit, return calls had to be made. One girl who attended at an Essex registry office early in the twentieth century remembered the sheer boredom of it: 'We had to ... stay there all day... It was weary and tiring spending days there'.

A number of unsatisfactory registries continued to exist, however, and in 1905 the London County Council, through its Public Control Committee, obtained powers to regulate the capital's agencies. None was to be approved if it accepted 'the name of any person known to be a prostitute or otherwise of ill-repute, or ... connected with a house of ill-fame' or 'knowingly transact business with such a person'.[41] Two years later the Council was authorised to carry out a licensing scheme and by the spring of 1909, of 573 agencies of all kinds formally registered, 430 dealt with domestic workers only and 88 more catered for governesses and servants. A report concluded that they appeared to 'exist in excess of public requirements, many such agencies being conducted by incompetent and unsuitable persons. Unsatisfactory and misleading methods of advertising have also been adopted by some of the agents'.[42]

Outside the capital public supervision was far more lax, with the option of exercising regulatory powers being left to individual local authorities under the permissive Public Health Amendment Act of 1907. Even by the early 1920s less than 5 per cent of authorities had adopted these powers. At that date it was claimed that only in London, Manchester, and Hull, plus the area covered by the Middlesex County Council, were effective controls in place to deal with third-rate or fraudulent agencies. It was very easy for dubious proprietors who had been driven out of London or Middlesex by the vigilance of the local authority to set up in business a few miles away in an unregulated district. A government report of 1923 pointed to cases where agents defrauded the public through bogus advertisements claiming to have efficient servants seeking situations on their books, or householders looking for staff. Many weekly provincial journals as well as London daily newspapers were used as vehicles for the false advertisements. The agents then pocketed the booking fees that employers and servants had sent to them in the hope of having their needs met. The report called for newspaper proprietors to refuse to publish advertisements of whose bona fides they had doubts.[43]

Nevertheless during the 1920s and 1930s registry offices were increasingly used as a way of hiring staff, with the number of those listed in the *London Post Office Trade Directory* growing from 88 in 1925 to 109 in 1939. In addition, many smaller agencies did not advertise in the directory at all. Some stayed in business for a short time only, but during the depression years between the wars a number of the more dubious organisations concentrated on bringing girls by train or motor-coach from areas of high unemployment to fill vacancies in London. Wales and the North-East of England were the main sources of supply. Most of the girls, however, lacked domestic experience, and the posts to which they were sent were often unsuitable. This unregulated traffic in what were often young teenagers caused concern among the leaders of the National Vigilance Association (NVA). This had been formed in 1885 to suppress 'criminal vice and public immorality' and one of its aims in the 1920s and 1930s was to prevent girls sent to unsuitable employment from drifting into prostitution or finding themselves homeless in the capital. To this end, NVA helpers were based at the main London railway termini and coach stations to be on hand to advise and assist youngsters who seemed to be at a loss and for whom the agencies had made no proper provision. The Victorian London website http://www.victorianlondon.org/ contains examples of the National Vigilance Society's early enquiries into the conditions and abuses of women who answered advertisements from such registries.

In 1935 F.A.R. Sempkins, the Association's secretary, wrote an article in the popular magazine, *Tit-Bits*, warning youngsters from the 'distressed areas' of the problems they could face. 'Imagine what it must feel like to be a ... girl of fourteen or so, with no experience of the world, no money and few clothes, arriving at a rail or coach station ... for the first time and being stranded there. That has happened to hundreds of girls from ... Wales and the North during the past few years; it is happening now every week'.[44] He claimed that during the previous year the Association had helped almost five thousand girls, mostly from Wales and Tyneside, who had arrived at London stations. At Paddington, where one helper was based, she had been almost overwhelmed by the large number of applications for help.

The NVA's own records confirm the validity of these warnings. One of the many offending registries was Mrs. Nicholls' Agency based in South Shields, but which also apparently traded under the name of the Clayton Agency at Newcastle-on-Tyne. Case studies show that one victim was fifteen-year-old Ivy Dawson from Ashington in Northumberland. She arrived at Kings Cross on 1 February 1936 and was contacted by an NVA helper. At that stage she did not seem to need help, as the daughter of the elderly lady who had hired her arrived to pick her up. However, four days later the girl returned with her suitcases and told the helper that her mother had sent the fare for her to return home. Apparently instead of being taken to the mother's house the daughter had taken Ivy to her own home. There the girl discovered the house was very dirty and she had so much to do that she could not get to bed until midnight. Doubtless her own inexperience added to the problem and so she decided to return home. The NVA caseworker took her to the appropriate motor-coach and she expressed her gratitude for the aid she had received. Not surprisingly, Ivy resolved never to return to London.[45]

Employers, too, were often dissatisfied with the sulky and incompetent girls sent to them. Mr. and Mrs. Blackman, who ran a tobacconist's shop in Lambeth Walk, recruited sixteen-year-old Ada Wilkinson from Sunderland in 1934 through the Clayton Agency. Mrs. Blackman complained that Ada did not know how to clean a house and was idle. When she approached the Agency they declared 'that all their responsibility ended from the moment they put [the girl] on the coach for London'. According to the report of the NVA caseworker, the Blackmans had paid the agency a fee of 12s. 6d. [62½p], plus the girl's fare. 'These agencies', the caseworker added, 'make on the fares as well, because I have been told by one of the bus inspectors, that [the] independent coaches ... give the domestic agencies a very big commission in order to get the girls', although the fare quoted to the employer was, of course, the standard one. The NVA's representative interviewed the parties and in the end Ada was taken by her to a hostel known to the Association until she got her return fare from home.[46] In other cases, employers claimed that the agencies persuaded the girls to change their posts quickly so that they could gain extra fees.[47]

The records of the London County Council show that even the capital's registry offices were not without their problems, as in September 1930 when an investigation revealed that an agency called the Woman's Exchange had demanded excessive fees from employers for servants coming from abroad. In this case the agent was cautioned about a possible loss of licence and agreed to refund £1 4s. 10d., which was the amount overcharged on rail fares. In another case, in July 1930 the Chalk Farm Agency was said to have made no attempt to supply a maid to the complainant although a booking fee had been paid. The agency excused itself by claiming that the low wage offered and the demands of the holiday season had prevented a suitable applicant being provided. However, the County Council inspector noted that well below half of all the employers who had paid fees to this agency were actually suited.[48]

Most registries, though, were reputable and some, like the Regina and the Mayfair in London, had a high-class clientele. The Mayfair had separate entrances for employers and servants, and Lily Milgate entered the wrong one by mistake. She was amazed at the elegant scene that greeted her: 'white and gold paint, velvet curtains and delicate chairs and sofas piled with cushions. I just stood on the thick carpet and stared until a very smart woman came sailing towards me. She knew at once'.[49] Lily was immediately sent next door. 'My word what a different scene this was. No thick carpet here, or velvet curtains ... The floor was covered with brown linoleum, benches lined each side of the room, one side for maids, the other for menservants ... I sat down to await my turn'.

Finally there were the government's labour exchanges, which were open to all workers. However, they played little part in filling private domestic vacancies. Their main contribution during the 1920s and 1930s was in filling seasonal posts during the summer months at seaside resorts and providing hotel and boarding house staff.[50] Both mistresses and maids preferred the specialist services of the private registries, despite the undoubted problems associated with some of them.

Training

The majority of girls entering domestic service received their initial training on the job from their mistress or a fellow servant, or they were instructed by their mother before they left home. But given the impoverished condition of many working-class homes, they had little experience of performing many of the tasks expected of them by the middle-class families who usually hired them.

Some philanthropic ladies, like Anne Sturges-Bourne and the Countess of Macclesfield, set up their own modest training schools to prepare mainly local girls for service. Lady Macclesfield's school was near her home at Shirburn Castle in Oxfordshire and was opened in January 1865. It catered for girls aged between twelve and sixteen, who remained at the school for up to three years. They were expected to be able to read and write on admission and were instructed in cooking, housework and laundry work, this latter having its commercial aspect. They washed not only articles supplied by the Castle itself but by gentry families in the district. These were charged for at 'the prices usual in the country' and provided an income for the school. Any spare time the girls had was devoted to needlework and to reading, writing and arithmetic, while religious instruction was given on the Sabbath and once during the week. In the first two and a half years of the school's existence, twelve girls were sent to service, each being supplied with an outfit by Lady Macclesfield before they embarked on their new career.[51]

As well as small ventures of this kind, as we have seen, poor law schools, reformatories and charitable institutions like the Foundling Hospital offered some rudimentary instruction in domestic work, usually of a rough and ready kind. In addition, in the years immediately before World War I specialist domestic service and domestic economy schools were set up by a few local authorities, although in 1914 their numbers remained tiny. There were just ten domestic service schools, four of them in the London area, and they had a total of around 350 students. Of the eighteen domestic economy schools, twelve of them were also in the capital. They had the broader objective of training girls as home-makers rather than merely as maids, but in 1914 they had fewer than seven hundred pupils, and during the First World War even that paltry number declined sharply.

The Girls' Friendly Society also established a training programme for members from the 1880s and in 1914 it introduced a Scheme for Standardisation, designed to provide certificates for girls who had completed a course of training successfully at a GFS Lodge or training home. The aim was to improve efficiency and to raise the status of domestic workers, but even when expanded in the 1920s its role remained small, with just 552 girls having completed its Junior and Preliminary examinations by 1929, and a mere sixty-nine having obtained the full qualification.[52]

It was left to the government through the Central Committee on Women's Training and Employment (CCWTE) in the years after the First World War to draw up a formal training programme. Its purpose was two-fold. During the War around four hundred thousand maids had left domestic service for war work, and when peace was restored many were unwilling to return to their old employment. In addition, there were younger women who had gone straight from school into factories and who had had no experience of household employment. One objective of the CCWTE scheme, at a time of high female unemployment, was to take as many as possible off the 'dole' and train (or retrain) them for domestic work. Secondly, there was a desire to satisfy the demands of middle-class householders for servants and to refute claims that the girls were 'scroungers' who were unwilling to work.

From 1921, therefore, the CCWTE began offering non-residential courses, each lasting for around three months and designed to fit trainees for domestic careers. About thirty hours of instruction were provided weekly in cookery, laundry work, needlework, and housewifery, together with lessons on hygiene and some general subjects. During the course the women received a weekly maintenance allowance of £1, from which they had to contribute 3s. (15p) towards the cost of the materials they used to make their uniforms ready for their future employment. By the end of the 1930s at least 85,000 women and girls had passed through the training programme. However, numbers fluctuated from year to year according to the state of the economy, general government policy, and the opportunities open to women to enter other, more attractive employment, rather than domestic service. In factory areas such as Lancashire and Cheshire there was a marked reluctance to take up the training courses, unless forced to do so by threats to withdraw their 'dole' money if they did not conform. In the cotton towns of the North-West of England resident domestic service was regarded with dislike 'as the last resource' of the average woman worker.[53] So, while there were 113 Home Training courses in operation in 1926, by 1928 that had fallen to 95 in the nation at large, held in forty-two different towns. From the late 1920s residential centres also began to appear, to cater for those unable to attend a day scheme, and in 1931 there were five of these open in various parts of Britain.

Initially, many of the centres were opened only temporarily, to meet a short-term rise in local female unemployment. At Workington in Cumbria, for example, a course was opened in May 1925 but it had very limited success, so that of sixty-one girls leaving in December 1925, only nineteen became maids, and six of these went as local day servants. The rest dropped out, took up other posts, were dismissed as unsuitable, or had not been confirmed in a situation even though they had been put in touch with an employer. Twenty-nine of the trainees were former mill workers and fourteen ex-shop assistants. Among the successes was a former carriage cleaner, aged twenty-eight, who became a housemaid in a Keswick hotel and a seventeen-year-old ex-colliery screen-hand who became a maid-of-all-work at 10s. a week. As a result of this limited support, the scheme was ended late in 1925, only to be revived in 1929 when unemployment again rose.[54]

The centres were located in the depressed areas where women had difficulty in finding alternative work. By the end of 1930, therefore, there were twelve in Durham and Tyneside and twelve in South Wales, with others located in Lanarkshire, Wigan, Workington, Leeds and Sheffield, making a total of thirty-seven in all. A few centres, like Ystrad in the Rhondda specialised in training juveniles under eighteen. During the three months ended on 18 September 1928, seventeen girls completed their course at Ystrad, none of them being over eighteen years. Nine of them had never been employed previously, five had been daily domestics before embarking on the course, two had previously been servants, and one had been a bottle washer. The rates of pay they commanded ranged from £20 to £25 per annum. Two of them - Amy West, aged sixteen and Eileen Lawrence, aged seventeen - obtained posts as cooks, which would seem to have been an act of faith on the part of some mistresses.[55]

Information on trainees at the South Shields centre was particularly detailed. Of thirty-nine women and girls on the course ending 12 June, 1933, thirty-five went into domestic posts. Surviving records list not only their previous employment and the kind of domestic post they wished to take up, but their height, their religious affiliation, whether they were willing to work outside their home area, and the location of the post they eventually took up. So, on a course ending 7 January, 1931, we learn that J. Hunter of South Shields was aged seventeen, was a Protestant and had formerly been employed as a fried fish shop assistant. She was 5 ft. 4 in. tall and was described as a 'nice type'. She took a general servant's place in Macclesfield. One of her fellow trainees, G. McGirvie, aged nineteen, was a Roman Catholic bakery worker, about 5 ft. 2 in. in height and of a 'sturdy appearance'. She went to work at the Royal Naval School, Twickenham.[56] Such records provide useful information for those seeking to trace relatives who may have been on such courses.

Some trainees had mixed fortunes when they embarked on their domestic career. Doris Clarke from South Shields was a twenty-two-year-old former shop assistant, who was sent to work for the Metcalfe family at The Old Hall, Threshfield. She remained for a few weeks only, finding the work too hard, the hours too long, and being faced at times with cooking for eleven people. It was recognised that this was too much for a raw recruit to undertake. Doris found a new post for herself not far from Threshfield and settled down happily for a time. But the place proved too isolated, and after some weeks she left there as well.[57]

During the 1930s special emphasis was placed on the training of younger girls, particularly from areas of high unemployment, and by 1934 youngsters under the age of fifteen were being admitted to three centres in South Wales. Their courses

Figure 16. Trainees learning new cooking skills at the Oxford Centre of the National Institute of Houseworkers, June 1949. (TUC Library).

were longer, lasting up to nine months in some cases, and none was sent to a post below the age of fifteen. As a result of these changes over 80 per cent of the girls attending domestic training centres at the end of 1935 were under eighteen years of age, and eight of the centres now took trainees under fifteen.[58]

As for the youngsters themselves, most took up domestic work because there was no alternative, although many found the courses enjoyable. Irene Thompson, born in Middlesbrough in 1918, came to a residential centre at Market Harborough, Leicestershire, when she was fourteen. She learnt of the course from a neighbour's daughter who also joined it. There were about forty girls in all, aged from fourteen to seventeen. 'They were very strict but we were happy', Irene recalled. 'On the whole I think we were glad enough to get away from home and the poverty and everything. [59] After she left she went to work for a retired bank manager and his wife in Leicester. The wife was a strict disciplinarian and she disliked Irene's north country accent. 'If I was serving dinner, she'd say "Now, say that again Irene", so I used to have to repeat it in her manner ... She always used to come in about ten to one and she'd go and inspect every job she'd given you, wiping all the picture rails and tops of the doors with her finger, [to] make sure I'd done them'.[60]

The training given during these years was intended to increase the supply of servants and to improve their standing, so as to establish domestic service as a skilled occupation, rather than one of last resort for those who could obtain no other work. This philosophy applied again after the Second World War when the government intervened once more to set up a domestic training scheme. The new organisation was the National Institute of Houseworkers (NIH), a title designed to avoid the use of the word 'servant' and to meet the post-war demand for efficient domestic workers. Its aim was to show that 'houseworkers' provided an 'essential community service' in an occupation that ought to be 'entirely honourable and self-respecting'.[61] Just as nursing had been transformed from a low status job in the nineteenth century to a profession enjoying considerable prestige by the mid-twentieth century, so it was hoped that by providing training, certification, and agreed working conditions, particularly as regards wages and hours of employment, the position of domestic work would be similarly changed. As skilled practitioners the women would themselves gain greater confidence and thereby break down the notion that domestic staff formed 'a race apart'. The training programme covered practical household tasks as well as some general and health education. The NIH began work in 1947 with the aim of boosting the supply of residential servants but it also made provision to supply daily helpers, who would work for individual families on an hourly basis.

Around two-thirds of the trainee's time was devoted to practical work and a further one-fifth to general education. The rest of the course involved working in specially selected private households. For those aged seventeen and above a six-months' course was envisaged, and for juveniles one of nine months. After this, the trainees went out as pre-diploma students to spend a year working in a household selected by the NIH, before returning to sit their examination.

By the end of 1949 nine centres were open, with places for 365 students. But it was also possible for 'experienced' domestic workers to take the certificate examination without attending a course. In the event, a majority of the successful candidates came from this background. In December 1960, when the scheme had been running for over a decade, only 1,537 of the 5,287 holders of the diploma had actually been on a training course.[62]

In May 1948 *The Houseworker*, the Institute's journal, included contributions from some of the successful workers, giving reasons why they had sought a formal qualification. One who had been a domestic worker for seven years thought it 'established a guarantee of my experience and also that it would be a very nice thing to have'. Another woman, employed as a cook-housekeeper by a semi-invalid, felt it would be 'a trump card to use', should she need to find fresh employment.

However, it is clear that most women employed as domestic servants, charwomen or home helps were not affected by this attempt to raise the status of their occupation. Indeed, the NIH's hopes of success were undermined by the disintegration of the domestic world it had been designed to support. Female job opportunities increased rapidly in the post-war years and the number of women and girls working as servants shrank. As early as 1953 seven of the nine residential centres were closed and by the early 1970s, at a time of financial cutbacks, the government decided to close down the whole enterprise. Household employment was destined to remain the province of the uncertificated practitioner who learnt on the job, just as it had always been. In January 1971, as part of a campaign by NIH leaders to preserve the Institute, it was pointed out that it was the only national organisation seeking to increase the supply of qualified domestic staff. It was ready to extend its remit to cater for domestic workers in hospitals and home helps employed by local authorities. [63] But the Government was unmoved, a Minister noting that the annual grant it was receiving 'could no longer be justified'. It was also pointed out that local authorities and other major employers of domestic workers, such as hospitals and hotels, had already developed their own training programmes. These largely replaced the NIH provision. By the autumn of 1972 the organisation had been finally wound up.[64]

For those who may have relatives who took part in this post-war scheme, lists of the women and girls who passed the certificate examination were published in some of the NIH's annual reports, and both they and its journal, *The Houseworker*, include contributions from individual participants, expressing satisfaction with their training or the improved status they had gained through the Institute's work. They included women like Rosemary Russell, who worked in a doctor's household in the London area. Her comments were included in the annual report for 1958-59 and she maintained that domestic work was more interesting than employment in a shop or a factory. She particularly enjoyed cooking, since this gave 'plenty of scope for change'.

But in the second half of the twentieth century few women were prepared to follow her example. Increasingly it was public institutions, like hospitals or residential homes, and the hospitality industry that became the main employers of domestic staff, rather than private householders. At most, the majority of these relied on the services of a 'daily' helper or a contract cleaner. Only the most affluent householders had live-in servants and child care providers, like nannies and mother's helps.

Those resident domestics who survived had to be multi-taskers in most cases. Arthur Inch who returned to service in the mid-1950s, after a break during the Second World War and its aftermath, found himself 'covering the jobs of ten men in the pantry... As well as being butler/valet I also did a few chauffeuring jobs such as taking the children to school'. Similarly a long-serving butler at a substantial property in south Leicestershire claimed in the mid-1980s that he could not name a place in the whole county that still had two full-time resident servants. 'After the War', he declared, 'you couldn't get men and women for domestic service and you started to get foreign staff as things began to go down.'[65] It was the end of an era.

CHAPTER FIVE
Social Relationships

Leisure and Pleasure

The social life of domestic servants was influenced by the kind of household in which they worked - whether they were single-handed maids-of-all-work or members of a large establishment - as well as by the attitude of employers, their own gender, and whether or not they were resident. If they lived out they could choose how to spend their time away from work, and during the 1920s and 1930s increasing numbers of domestics did live out. According to the 1931 Census of Population for England and Wales, of the 78,489 males and 1,332,224 females classed as indoor servants, almost a quarter of the men and two-fifths of the women and girls were non-resident.[1] In addition, just over half of the females in private service were in one-servant households. By contrast, in Victorian times, although single-handed maids were common the majority of both male and female domestics lived on their employer's premises. This led to a feeling of being 'under orders all day' and of never being 'off duty'.[2] In 1916 an Enquiry published by the Women's Industrial Council concluded that most of the servants contacted had identified 'lack of liberty' as the dominant reason why domestic work had become increasingly unpopular as an occupation.[3]

Females were particularly restricted, partly on moral grounds to prevent them from striking up unsuitable friendships if they were allowed unlimited freedom. In 1887 the Annual Report of the Girls' Friendly Society drew attention to the evils that could arise from permitting young servants working in towns to have evenings out. It noted that in some places the Society itself had opened club rooms where members without family or friends in the locality could spend their free evenings 'safely and pleasantly'.[4] One club, established in the St. Pancras area of London, offered tea, a lending library and a savings bank, as well as companionship. The GFS also criticised mistresses who insisted that their maids spend their free afternoons and evenings away from the house. In some cases the girls were locked out when the employers themselves went visiting.

Even the Domestic Servants' Association combined its friendly society work during the First World War with the setting up of clubs, with seventeen branches in existence by April 1915. Most were in the London area but a few were in the provinces, including in Bath, Birmingham, Bristol, Manchester and Norwich. Meetings offered dancing, games and, in the summer excursions and communal picnics.[5]

A few years later a new edition of Mrs. Beeton's *Book of Household Management* emphasised that a mistress 'should never allow herself to forget the important duty of watching over the moral and physical welfare of those beneath her roof. Without seeming unduly inquisitive she can always learn something of their acquaintances and holiday occupation, and should, when necessary, warn them against the dangers and evils of bad company'.[6] But to many of the girls this seemed an unwarranted invasion of their privacy, especially when their spare time was so limited.

On occasion, as with the irascible early nineteenth century Somerset clergyman, John Skinner, the restrictions were carried further. In October 1821 Skinner noted disapprovingly that one of his maids had 'entangled herself in a village connection ... How often have I warned my servants from forming any acquaintance with the people around me, as it is sure to involve them in mischief. Indeed I have made it a rule when I hire a servant to state my dislike of their going into the village, but promised in lieu to permit them at stated times to go home to their friends, or occasionally to see them here.'[7]

In large households the senior staff issued the warnings and imposed the restraints, under the overall direction of their employers. One housekeeper at a substantial property near St. James's Park in London noted that the nursemaids were 'not supposed to visit the Park, as they generally do, without someone to attend them - on account of Red Coats and Music which are tempting things to inexperienced girls'.

"HA! HA! THE WOOIN' O'T!"—*Old Song.*

Young Mistress (gravely ; she had seen an affectionate parting at the garden-gate).
"I SEE YOU'VE GOT A YOUNG MAN, JANE!"

Jane (apologetically). "ONLY WALKED OUT WITH HIM ONCE, M'UM!"

Mistress. "O, BUT I THOUGHT I SAW—DIDN'T YOU—DIDN'T HE—TAKE A KISS,
JANE?"

Jane. "O, M'M, ONLY AS A FRIEND, M'M!!"

*Figure 17. Maid being questioned by her mistress about a meeting with her 'young man'.
The usual rule was 'no followers allowed'. (Punch, 1871)*

It was feared they would form unwelcome liaisons with soldiers and be tempted into prostitution. John Gillis suggests that former servants may have made up between a third and a half of London prostitutes in the nineteenth century.[8] But even in the 1920s a housemaid at Thornby Hall, Northamptonshire, remembered: 'You had to be in at ten or else the old cook-housekeeper came out of her sitting-room.'[9]

From the later Victorian years servants increasingly felt that their own social standing also affected their leisure activities, with many complaining that their occupation was despised by members of their own class in other employment. As a lady's maid in her mid-thirties, member of a household of eight domestics, told the 1916 Enquiry by the Women's Industrial Council: 'Once a servant you are treated as belonging to quite an inferior race to all other workers; it is as if the lowest point has been reached.' Similarly a cook from London, also in her thirties, confessed that when she went to the seaside on holiday and boarded with 'a number of business girls, I never enlighten them as to how I earn my living', so as to avoid losing caste.[10] Unfortunately their work-roughened hands often betrayed their secret. But the point was perhaps made most clearly by a parlourmaid in the 1920s when she complained that invitations out often stated: 'Be sure and do not let it be known you are a domestic. We should not like our friends to mix with servants.' This feeling of inferiority was aggravated by the 'constant caricaturing of maidservants' in the press, as well as by the mocking portrayals of them by dramatists and cartoonists. These attacks and witticisms were keenly felt and resented by the girls, as was the use of contemptuous terms like 'skivvy' and 'slavey' when referring to them.[11]

Such sensitivities applied particularly to urban servants and those in small households, since staff working for well-established landed families often gained reflected glory from their employers' superior social position. 'Farmers and small tradesmen', declared one writer on the rural community, 'look up to the housekeeper and butler', and regarded themselves 'on a level with the ordinary servants in a great house.[12]

But there was the snobbishness of employers to contend with, too. Mrs. Timms of Chadlington in Oxfordshire was a victim of this. In the 1920s she worked for a comfortably-off widow and wished to learn the piano and to play tennis, but her mistress disapproved. 'Whoever heard of a domestic servant wanting to do such things', she declared, 'what would my father have said'? Mrs. Timms added wryly: 'Her father was a clergyman in the 1880s.' But she made the best of things, spending her free time sketching or riding round the countryside on her bicycle. She also cleaned the brasses in the parish church on her weekly half-day, seemingly of her own volition.[13] Her enjoyment of the freedom given by ownership of a bicycle

Figure 18. Maids enjoying a tea party in the garden of Garsington Rectory, Oxfordshire, in the 1890s. (Centre for Oxfordshire Studies and Oxfordshire County Council Photographic Archive).

was shared by Mrs. Slade. She worked for a minor landed family in Kent and described cycling as her 'only pleasure'. She bought her bicycle on hire-purchase, taking two years to clear the debt.

The amount of leisure servants enjoyed varied widely and in the early and mid-Victorian years could be very limited indeed, especially for those in single-handed places. Male servants were usually more fortunate in that they were often sent out with messages or on errands, and were then able to extend these to their own advantage. Or, as with William Tayler, the footman employed by the Prinsep family in London in 1837, they could slip out in the morning or afternoon once their principal tasks were completed. 'Went out this morning, staid a long time,' noted Tayler in his diary on 5 May. 'When I came home, the maidservants grumbled very much because I left them to answer all the doors and bells.' But this did not deter him, for two days later he wrote: 'Took a walk in the Park before breakfast, found it very pleasant'.[14] On other occasions he visited friends and relatives, including his wife and children, of whose existence his mistress was quite ignorant, or entertained his friends in the Prinseps' kitchen. In the 1890s Lady Violet Greville considered that male servants spent too much time in public houses or in one of the many servants' clubs which were established in the capital. 'Clubs are an immense institution and a great resort of servants', she declared. However, her reference to public houses was significant, since an over-fondness for drink and gambling were weaknesses particularly associated with butlers, footmen and coachmen. Butlers were also well placed to sample the contents of their employer's cellar, since decanting wine and maintaining a check on the supplies of alcohol were part of the duties of most of them.

Outdoor male servants, such as gardeners, stable workers and gamekeepers were better situated, in that their working hours were usually more regular than for their indoor counterparts and their evenings were free. On large estates employers often provided a club house and sporting facilities for their staff. Tom Spuggard, whose father was a woodman on the Cliveden estate between the two World Wars, remembered there were staff football and cricket teams, as well as fortnightly dances in the club room and annual events like a sports day and a Christmas party. There was a bowling alley, too. But few of these activities were 'democratic', in that they took place under the shadow of the big house, both at Cliveden and at other stately homes.[15]

The clandestine comings and goings of indoor male servants like William Tayler may be contrasted with the tighter regime that applied to female staff like Mrs. Layton of Bethnal Green. She first went out as a maid-of-all-work in Hampstead at the age of thirteen in 1868 and was only allowed time off on Sundays to go to church. That meant she was unable to visit her family, so sometimes she played truant, and instead of going to church she went to see a married sister who lived about a mile away. 'This meant I had to run all the way there and back to enable me to stay for a very short time with my sister.' From there she went to a family in Kentish Town, where she was allowed time off on Sundays between 3 pm and 5 pm one week and from 6.30 pm to 9 pm the next. She spent most of this going for walks. Her third place was with a widow and her daughter and this time the mistress allowed her to go out every evening between 7.30 pm and 9 pm. In that household, too, unlike in her previous places, she was encouraged to read. Books were lent to her and she was helped to improve her basic education by writing out sentences which her mistress then corrected for spelling and grammar.[16]

In these small places servants' day-to-day social encounters were mostly limited to tradespeople making deliveries or workmen carrying out repairs on the premises, or perhaps people they met when going on errands. An unofficial 'recreation' indulged in by some of them was to eavesdrop on the private conversations of their employers, perhaps by listening outside closed doors. In the enforced intimacy of domestic life they learned many family secrets, which they might pass on to fellow servants they met on their days off, when the merits and demerits of mistresses were discussed.

In large establishments the strict staff hierarchy and the careful division of labour meant there was normally a clearer allocation of free time. But much depended on the amount of entertaining that took place. When George Slingsby went as a hall boy to Rufford Abbey in the early 1900s the housekeeper told him that his duties would begin at 6 am each day and that he would have 'no set working hours'. When the family entertained he might be on call until midnight. However, he would have one weekend off every month and one other free day every fortnight. He would be at liberty in the evening after his work was finished, but must be sure to be in by midnight. He was allowed to attend morning service at church on Sundays if he wished.[17]

Formal holidays lasting for several days were more problematic. William Lanceley remembered having a holiday after four years' service when the family for whom he was working went away on a round of visits lasting six weeks. But 'no servant would dream of asking for one unless the family were away from home ... My first holiday was three days, quite enough at that time. Our cottage homes and food were no comparison to what we had left behind'.[18] Not all servants were so philosophical. Indeed, when Rose Gibbs, who worked for a landed family near Dorking, asked for a day off so she could go to London to see her mother, she was told that if she did so she would lose her place. Outings into Dorking for half a day were permitted but longer excursions were not. In these circumstances, Rose decided to resign, even though in other respects she was happy in the household.[19] As Arthur Inch, who served in a number of large households between the wars, commented: 'We never used to get regular holidays in service.' When he worked at West Wycombe Park in Buckinghamshire during the 1930s he did not get even a weekend off until he had been there for fifteen months. The staff rarely had a free Sunday, as there were nearly always week-end parties 'and it was a case of all hands to the pump'. They were officially allowed one half-day a week after lunch, but had to be back by 10 pm and there were occasional free evenings if the Dashwoods, who owned West Wycombe Park, were away. 'There wasn't a lot to do except the cinema in High Wycombe or the occasional dance in the village hall and where we, from the Park, would go with some of the housemaids and kitchen staff. We would all go down together and back again after the dance ... Very occasionally if finances were good I would take a trip to London and see a show or a good film ... or look at some of the notable landmarks'.[20] But Arthur wanted to visit his family in Yorkshire and so, like Rose Gibbs, he handed in his notice, resolving to go north for a week or two before seeking another post. Other servants adopted a similar strategy if they wanted to have a holiday. It was, of course, unpaid leave.

In 1919, a government report concluded that a reduction in the length of the working day and more free time were essential if domestic service were to be made attractive. To that end it suggested there should be a free half-day every Sunday, plus an afternoon and evening off during the week. On other days a minimum of two hours should be set aside when the worker could go out or remain in the house, but would not be expected to answer bells or carry out any other tasks. A fortnight's paid holiday should be allowed each year, and a half-day or more allocated at Bank Holidays.[21] This ideal was rarely achieved in the 1920s and 1930s. In fact when the National Institute of Houseworkers (NIH) specified in the late 1940s and the 1950s that employers recruiting a maid from their training courses should restrict her hours to ninety-six per fortnight, unless she agreed to put in paid overtime, there was immediate resistance. Mistresses felt that if a girl were on the premises, perhaps reading or sewing in her room, she should be available for work. But the NIH argued it was important to recognise that, as in other occupations, there should be regular leisure time. During these 'off duty' periods the maid should be 'free to stay in the house, which is her home, as well as her place of employment, without having duties ... imposed upon her'. To employers this appeared too much of a 'trade union' approach and, as such, was not appropriate within a domestic setting, no matter how much it might be accepted in other spheres of work.[22]

In single-handed places servants rarely had anywhere except a sparsely furnished kitchen in which to spend their free time. Leisure activities within the home were usually limited to reading, sewing and knitting, although when wind-up gramophones and later wirelesses became available some were allowed to have these. But the amount of time they could spend listening was usually restricted. Irene Thompson, when working for a retired bank manager and his wife in Leicester, remembered only being allowed to have her radio on at teatime, 'when they had Henry Hall, which I loved being a young girl, dance music'. She was given Sunday evenings off provided she went to church first. 'Funnily enough, that's where I met my husband, as we came out of church one night.' As with most households, however, there was a strict rule of 'no followers' allowed, so she was not permitted to meet him at the house: 'he had to wait at the end of the road or somewhere'.[23]

Even the girls' reading material was subjected to critical comment, especially in the Victorian and Edwardian periods, when their fondness for 'penny dreadfuls' was condemned. At the 1889 annual conference of the Girls' Friendly Society its Literature Department discussed, 'How to guard GFS Members against the evils of cheap, bad literature'. One speaker deplored the practice of distributing cheap books with packets of 'bonus' tea, and others urged that when a member joined the GFS she should be warned 'against reading police reports and divorce cases' in the newspapers. 'It would often be a help to a girl to be able to say, "I belong to a Society that forbids the reading of evil in books and papers".'[24] It is unlikely that many members took notice of these solemn pronouncements.

Within stately homes, on the other hand, despite the divisions between upper and lower servants, friendships did develop between the staff. One woman recalled that in her grandmother's Welsh home between the wars there were 'gales of laughter coming from down in the kitchen ... If they wanted fresh air, they could walk round the garden, ... often with their knitting as they strolled about (but not in the front garden!)'[25] There were opportunities, too, for gossip, sing-songs and even impromptu dances. But in the restricted conditions of life below stairs there could also be quarrels. Grace Germany, employed by Vanessa Bell at her Sussex home, noted in her diary in March 1922 that she had almost had 'a row' with the cook 'about my awful Socialist views. Mrs. Harland thinks that the poorer classes never ought to be allowed to get into parliament. I think that the poor are on the same level as the rich & some superior in Brains ... & she also says I am mad, because I said I do not want to get married, as I would lose my independence'. Later she had strained relations with Alice, another of the maids, partly, it would seem, because of Alice's coarse conversation and the fact that she was a frequent visitor to the local public house. When Alice eventually left in October 1924, Grace noted drily:

'She has taken my ring & a pound. Alas poor me. It says always pay debts & Compliments & you will succeed. *May Alice succeed.*'[26]

Far more dramatic was the quarrel between one of Mrs. Disraeli's housekeepers, Mrs. Rogers, and a maid, when the latter was reproved for not giving the cats the correct amount of milk. The maid responded by calling her 'a lying Bald Old Devvel', and throwing a glass of beer over her. This was followed by a physical attack in which the housekeeper was seized by the shoulders and shaken violently: 'feeling alarm I scream'd Murder - not satisfied she then threw a cup of tea over me - all this I thank God without [my] raising a hand.'[27] After the encounter Mrs. Rogers decided to leave. Earlier, in May 1857, the Disraelis' then butler, Mr. Richardson, was dismissed for fighting with the coachman at Hughenden, their country estate in Buckinghamshire.[28]

Flirtations inevitably took place where male and female servants were employed in the same household, despite the firm prohibitions upon any intimacy between indoor staff. The flouting of these rules could lead to immediate discharge. The Disraeli household was affected by this, too, when in April 1855 Mrs. Disraeli discovered that John Haynes, the under-butler, had been behaving improperly 'about 2 women', one of whom was the cook and the other a maid. He was immediately dismissed, even though he had worked in the household for nearly three years. The fact that he already had a wife and child may have been a deciding factor. Interestingly, neither of the female servants lost her place, and some months later Benjamin Disraeli himself recommended Haynes to a friend as 'a capable, & very obliging, servant'.[29]

But the possibility of serious sanctions did not prevent servant intimacies, as the two sexes met each other in the servants' hall, at family prayers, in the course of their duties, and on their way to and from church or at the servants' dances and parties organised by employers in many large households. Eric Horne warned men-servants of the pitfalls that could follow 'canoodling' in the housemaids' cupboards, where they stored their pails and brushes, or in other dark corners away from 'the eagle eye of the housekeeper ... Don't blast your whole future for the sake of five minutes excitement'.[30]

Footmen had a reputation for womanising and the diary of Thomas, footman to the Duke and Duchess of Sutherland in the late 1830s, reveals he was no exception. The attentions he paid to the stillroom maid at Westhill, one of the Duke's residences, led to clashes with another footman. On other occasions he took out two of the maids, Anne and Sarah, either together or separately, for walks in the park, visits to the theatre and outings to Wandsworth Fair. However, when he took Sarah on a day trip to Chiswick, Anne was much offended because she had not been invited, and the trouble she caused seems to have ended their friendship. When Thomas tried to improve his knowledge of French by paying visits to the young French nursemaid, however, the housekeeper intervened. Instead he was allowed to have 'regular sessions with the more mature Madame Rousseau, one of the Duchess's personal maids'.[31] Card playing seems to have been a common pastime among the servants, both in the Duke's service and elsewhere, while Thomas was also involved in arranging impromptu dances. The porter at Trentham, another ducal property, played the violin, a second man-servant played the flute and Thomas himself performed on the clarinet, using it to provide dance tunes and purchasing sheet music for the purpose. As Pamela Sambrook notes, he appears to have been the instigator of many of the parties: 'All the lasses at West hill said they were very glad to see me return ... they had not had one dance all the time I had been away', he noted on one occasion.[32]

Formal staff dances were held at many stately homes, sometimes to celebrate special events, at others as part of the general routine of servant life. At Longleat, there were twice weekly dances held in the servants' hall, with a pianist engaged from neighbouring Warminster. A buffet supper was produced by the kitchen and stillroom staff, and the outdoor servants also attended, including the unmarried grooms and gardeners living in bothies. 'I like to think of those still room maids and housemaids discarding their printed chintz dresses and muslin caps for their evening finery,' wrote the Marchioness of Bath of these events. They then went down to the hall 'to dance with the "bothy" boys. The housekeeper would keep an eagle eye on the younger maids, noticing whom they danced with and reprimanding the over-frivolous.'[33]

At Christmas a grand servants' ball was given in the dining room, to which the local tradespeople who served the house were also invited. It was customary for the Marquess of Bath to open the ball with the housekeeper, while the Marchioness danced with the house steward. 'The Lancers was always the second dance'.[34]

At Westhill, there was a special Christmas dinner for the servants, with all the domestic staff and the outdoor labourers dining in the servants' hall, except for the most senior people, who dined in the steward's room, and the kitchen workers who ate in the kitchen. 'We had a very good dinner of roast beef and plum pudding and all a mince pie apiece and as much ale as we could drink', reported Thomas. Later the housemaids prepared tea, after which they played whist and cribbage until 1 am, when the housekeeper told them all to go to bed. But some of the men were reluctant to obey and they became so 'noisy and quarrelsome' that the housekeeper returned to remonstrate with them. That evening seems to have presaged 'a general falling out' among the staff, according to Thomas. 'The laundrymaids, the stillroom, Dairy and Betsy Housemaid were offended at the gardeners taking so much notice of the nursery maids and they all protested that they would not come in the hall on New Year's Eve', when other celebrations were anticipated. On 27 December Thomas accompanied the Westhill housemaids to a ball at Stafford House, the Duke's town house, where there was dancing to a violin until 3 am. But the New Year's Eve celebrations at Westhill seem to have been less successful with Betsy, the housemaid, and Sarah, from the dairy, telling the housekeeper about the alcohol that the gardeners were collecting cash to provide. Thomas was involved in sharing the drinks out: 'I made some grog, gin and water, brandy and water and rum, sherry and port ...' The dancing went on until 4 am and Thomas had to sleep in the servants' hall as someone else was occupying his bed. The reports of the event angered the housekeeper to such an extent that she threatened the gardeners with 'dismissal if they came up to the servants' hall again'. She later expressed her concern that there were quarrels among the staff and that they 'were not more united together'.[35]

But long-standing courtships among the servants occurred, too, as with Gerald Horne, who was a footman in a stately home in Devon in 1911. He fell in love with the head kitchenmaid, whom he later married. They circumvented the prohibitions on courtship by leaving notes for one another under the mat in the lamp room. Sometimes they rose at 4 am in order to sneak out for a walk in the woods, or they would slip out secretly for a few minutes in the evening.[36] Other servants overcame the restrictions in a similarly devious manner. Indeed, Stanley Sewell, who served as butler and footman in a number of country houses between the two World Wars, claimed that most male servants married fellow domestics, since they had little opportunity to meet other girls. 'Butlers always married a housemaid or a kitchenmaid, or a lady's maid sometimes.' He himself had married a lady's maid.[37] Maids, however, often married local labourers or artizans or outdoor workers, like gardeners and stable staff.

Serious recreational activities were provided in a few households, with libraries supplied and a piano installed in the servants' hall. William Lanceley, when working for the Duchess of Connaught, recalled that his mistress's fondness for music led her to encourage it in her staff. A piano was provided for their use. 'It was much appreciated,' wrote Lanceley, 'and in a very short time even the new-comers could play very well. A few took music lessons and these helped the others in their first attempts. There are always good singers to be found in large or small houses, and everyone knows that singing with music makes all the difference to a happy evening.'[38]

Few employers, however, carried their concern to 'improve' their servants as far as the Earl and Countess of Aberdeen. At their home, Haddo House, a club was formed, with an elected committee of eight to organise its activities, under the headings of Education and Recreation. Lord and Lady Aberdeen were the president and vice-president, and the other committee members were senior servants. Education was catered for by classes in elementary science, Bible study, composition and arithmetic, while books were made available in the bothies, stables and the gun-room. Two copies of the evening newspaper were placed in the library, with a rule that no club member could retain a copy for longer than ten minutes if another member required it. On the recreational side, dances were held and magic lantern shows arranged, but the singing class proved particularly successful.[39] When the Aberdeens moved between their residences, the servants' club arrangements went, too. However, their close involvement in many of these activities was regarded with disapproval by other members of High Society. They considered it blurred the traditional divide between Upstairs and Downstairs. Significantly, when the Earl was appointed Lord Lieutenant of Ireland, the King, Edward VII, on an official visit to Dublin, did not stay at Viceregal Lodge. Malicious gossip circulated that this was 'in case he found himself obliged to take a parlourmaid in to dinner', given the Aberdeens' somewhat unconventional attitude.[40] In the event this small social experiment ended with the outbreak of the First World War.

Many servants in grand households took a vicarious pleasure in witnessing their employers' lavish hospitality and seeing the important people they entertained, even if the glittering dinner parties and balls, or the country house visits meant extra work. For certain of the male servants and for housemaids who undertook some of the duties of a lady's maid, these house parties could prove lucrative, with tips being dispensed. When the Disraelis visited Hatfield House, home of the Marquess of Salisbury, for example, for weekend visits in the mid-1850s, their household accounts reveal tips of 10s. to the groom of the chambers and 5s. to a housemaid on such occasions.[41] Thomas, one of the Duke of Sutherland's footmen, also welcomed the tips he received, laying out some of the cash on purchases of fashionable clothes and boots. That included spending 5s. 9d. on a black silk cravat on one occasion.[42]

Although the custom of expecting tips had weakened by the end of the Victorian era it had certainly not disappeared. On the eve of the First World War, Frederick Gorst recalled the contempt with which one of the Duke of Portland's men-servants greeted a proposed tip of 6d. for sending a telegram: "'I couldn't possibly accept this," Hales said, drawing himself up to his full six foot three. "I suggest, Count

Apponyi, that you keep the sixpence. You might want to send another telegram." The Count flushed and said nothing. Then he dug in his pocket and presented Hales with a sovereign.'

Finally, for some fortunate servants, particularly valets and lady's maids, employment in a well-to-do family could offer the chance of foreign travel. In fact Rosina Harrison, who became Lady Astor's long-serving lady's maid, originally chose the occupation because she wanted to travel abroad. She was not disappointed.[43] Again, Charles Cooper, both as a footman and a butler, visited the South of France, acting as a courier for his employer. At the luxury hotel where they stayed at Cannes there was a special couriers' room where the visiting servants could meet. On one occasion, when there were about sixty maids, valets and chauffeurs staying in the hotel, a couriers' ball was held, with the dancing interspersed with singing, plenty of champagne and food from a well-stocked buffet.[44] Even in less affluent households there could be visits to the seaside in Britain itself or trips for shooting and fishing north of the border. William Tayler was one who enjoyed a lengthy stay at Brighton with the Prinseps in the summer of 1837.

Misfortunes, Misdoings and Misconduct

Apart from the problems caused by prolonged spells of unemployment and ill-health (at least before the 1911 National Insurance Act offered a modest sickness benefit and medical care), one of the greatest misfortunes to befall a maid was an unwanted pregnancy. The many hundreds of mothers' petitions preserved in the Foundling Hospital's archives, written to appeal for an illegitimate baby to be taken into the Hospital's care, attest to this. They also detail the events which had brought about this unhappy situation. Significantly, research by John Gillis indicates that taking the nineteenth century as a whole, about two-thirds of all the unmarried mothers whose children were admitted to the Hospital were in personal service. During the 1870s and 1880s that proportion was still higher. Similarly, of 371 single women admitted in 1880 to Queen Charlotte's Lying-in Hospital in London, 254 were servants. [45] This took place despite the fact that it was the policy at Queen Charlotte's to segregate unwed mothers from the rest and to allow them no visitors for ten days after the confinement. But begging a charity ticket to enter the Hospital was perhaps less humiliating than giving birth in a workhouse.[46]

The Foundling Hospital demanded written petitions so as to enable its officials to check on the mother's background and the likelihood that if she were relieved of the care of her child she would be able to be respectably re-employed. The accounts show that some of the women had been courting for several years and had been planning to marry when sexual intercourse took place. This was true of Anna Maria Darvill, who was a cook at Holwell Rectory near Hitchin and was aged twenty-four when she submitted her petition. She had given birth in November 1874, the child's father, Charles Bunter, being a house painter and the son of the rector's gardener. The couple had been engaged for over two years and Charles had visited the Darvill family on numerous occasions. One Sunday afternoon while the rector and his family were at church, he came into the kitchen and against Anna's will, sexual intercourse took place. It was not repeated but she became pregnant. When she told Bunter of this he suggested she have an abortion, which was not only illegal but was dangerous, and she indignantly refused. He subsequently left the area, his parents claiming to know nothing of his whereabouts. In August 1874, Anna left the rectory on the plea of ill health, without revealing her situation. She returned to her parents, and then went to an address in Chelsea to be confined. Despite pressure from the Darvill family and, allegedly, from his own mother, Bunter would not marry her. In the meantime Anna managed to get a new post with a Mr. Ripley in Kilburn. He knew nothing of her plight and she was anxious that he should remain in ignorance. Her former employer was then contacted and he confirmed that she had been a respectable servant. In these circumstances the Foundling Hospital agreed to take her little boy on 4 September, 1875, when he was almost ten months old.[47]

In other cases it was tradesmen who came to the door who courted the maids, despite the prohibition on 'followers'. That applied to Alice Tamplin, who became engaged to a milkman, Charles Middlemiss. After the engagement they had intercourse but then his mother's milk business failed and he became unemployed. He went away to look for work and although he wrote letters repeatedly promising to look after Alice and the baby, he did not do so. Alice, at the age of about nineteen, became an unmarried mother. She had lost her own mother while she was a baby and had been brought up by an aunt and uncle. She returned to the uncle's to live, concealing from her mistress the reason for her departure. She went to an address in Eastbourne to give birth to the child. Eventually she managed to find other employment with a couple who knew of her situation, and the eleven-month-old baby was accepted by the Foundling Hospital in March 1875.[48]

Sometimes the maids were seduced by fellow servants, including foreign workers, or they were subjected to sexual assault by a fellow domestic or a member of the mistress's family. Many of the girls were desperate to keep what they regarded as a shameful secret from their family, and went instead to the workhouse or spent their savings in seeking lodgings while they awaited the baby's birth. In certain cases, as with nineteen-year-old Elizabeth Finch, her parents flatly refused to have anything to do with the girl. In Elizabeth's case they claimed that if she returned home she would be a bad influence on their younger children. She had fallen victim to the blandishments of a Spanish groom who had been temporarily lodging with her master, and soon after she became pregnant he left the country. Elizabeth gave birth to her child at Paddington workhouse but was then able to find refuge with a distant relative. Her aim was to return to work as a maid if the baby were accepted by the Hospital. After due investigation, it was.[49]

But there were instances where the maid kept her condition a secret from everyone while she continued working and then gave birth alone, sometimes on her employer's premises. In these circumstances if the infant died it was often the result of an accident at the birth, perhaps due to the mother's panic and inexperience or to her losing consciousness at a crucial moment, or merely the result of lack of care during the pregnancy, rather than murder. Prison and court records detail some of these tragic cases. Where infanticide did occur, it may have been committed in a moment of desperation, when no other solution seemed possible and when the girl's prime concern was to hide the child's body. Fear of a loss of livelihood and reputation, or of becoming a social outcast, coupled with lack of resources to care for a child or of knowledge of where to go for help, may all have played a part. In 1852 Matilda Bunn, a servant suspected of murdering her baby, told Marylebone Police Court: 'if I had had friends to go to this would not have happened'.[50] In fact, according to one witness to the Capital Punishment Commission of 1866, infanticide was often committed 'to avoid the burden' of the baby's support. 'A large proportion of these cases are those of young women out in service', he added.[51]

After the birth some of the women amazingly seem to have returned to their duties as if nothing had happened. Even when evidence appeared to point to murder having taken place, the courts were reluctant to find the women guilty of infanticide, which could carry a death sentence. Instead they were accused of the lesser offence of concealing the birth, which under legislation passed in 1803, carried a maximum penalty of two years in prison. But many girls served far less than that. In one case, Ellen Trollope, a young maid working at a house in Earl's Court, London, gave birth to her illegitimate child alone in her room. She then cut the baby's throat and its skull was also fractured. Another servant heard her groans during the labour and later searched the room, finding the body of the newborn infant hidden in a chest. Despite the evidence of injury to the child, Ellen was acquitted of murder and served only two weeks in prison, without hard labour.[52]

A similarly lenient punishment was imposed on Rosanna Churchill, a dairymaid in her early twenties, whose baby had also died. She was employed at Upper Winchendon in Buckinghamshire and gave birth secretly. The father was from the parish of Soulbury, where she had worked the previous year as a maid to the local schoolmaster. According to the chaplain at Aylesbury gaol, where she was held to await trial, she initially seemed 'quite shameless'. She arrived in the gaol on 3 January 1854 but when she appeared before the Assizes two months later, the court let her off very lightly. She was sentenced to just one hour's imprisonment. That was, of course, in addition to the two months she had already served while awaiting the trial.[53]

It is worth noting that although nominally infanticide remained a capital offence, no woman was hanged for the murder of her own baby after 1849.[54]

Far more common than these cases, however, were crimes of petty peculation or systematic theft carried out by servants. The records of the courts, the prisons and the newspapers detail many such examples, although even more were probably not pursued through legal channels. Employers preferred to dismiss the recalcitrant servant, rather than engage in court proceedings. Cooks were particularly likely to be involved in these offences because of their ready access to food, which they could pass on to friends and relatives, or dispose of clandestinely to dealers. Margaret Thomas, when employed as a kitchen maid in a London household, remembered the cook there periodically despatched parcels of 'surplus' provisions to her own home. She also had commission from the tradesmen each month when the accounts were settled, and 'woe betide them if they didn't turn up with it; there were complaints about their goods until they did'.[55]

However, where employers were neglectful in their household management or unaware of the precise contents of their plate closets, they were particularly vulnerable to serious predations. These included butlers who pawned or sold some of the silver, perhaps to settle gambling debts. Barbara Charlton, mistress of Hesleyside in Northumberland, recalled ruefully how their long-serving butler proved 'a sly, plausible and cautious thief'. Not until he had been with the family for twenty-one years as footman and butler were his nefarious activities discovered, when he got drunk and made damaging revelations. It was found he had robbed the family of £40 in cash 'and several valuable articles besides'.[56]

Another master who had little interest in domestic detail was the sixth Duke of Devonshire. One of his attendants 'helped himself to £500 of the housekeeping money, and spent it on gambling'. In a further case a valet, who was a persistent drunkard, was finally dismissed after being found in a brothel. The deciding factor seems to have been that he took the Duke's dog with him to the brothel, and both were found there.[57] Another of his failures was to appoint a Miss Bicknell, who had worked at a local inn, as his housekeeper at Chatsworth. She soon took advantage of her position, ordering flowers and fruit for her friends and entertaining them at Hardwick House, another of the Duke's properties, with members of the Chatsworth staff waiting on them. Her fatal mistake was to hold a musical party in the Duke's private rooms, something which deeply angered him and led to her speedy dismissal.[58]

But most of the thefts and misdoings were more mundane than these examples. Often they seem to have been products of impulse or perhaps of envy on the part of servants who had few possessions of their own. They included girls like Ada Wood, aged sixteen, who stole a gold locket, valued at £3 10s. from her mistress in Slough. Ada came from a respectable family in London, her father being a clerk, and it was her first offence. However, when charged in November 1871 she was sentenced to two months' imprisonment with hard labour. The chaplain of Aylesbury gaol, where she was confined, concluded that although the crime was attributable to her 'bad disposition', her mistress 'deserved it for taking her without a character'.[59]

More desperate was the plight of thirteen-year-old Isabella Montgomery, charged in 1854 with stealing a sovereign. She had been born in Glasgow and had worked in a cotton factory there, earning 9s. a fortnight, until in the autumn of 1853 her uncle, who lived at Wolverton in Buckinghamshire, brought her south to act as a servant to him, his wife and their large family. She received no pay other than her board and lodging, and was overworked and 'cruelly beaten'. She stole the sovereign to pay her rail fare back to Glasgow and had got as far as Rugby when she was arrested. She was sentenced to one month's imprisonment with hard labour, but the chaplain at Aylesbury gaol was clearly touched by her story, for he wrote to her father, a Glasgow shoemaker, presumably to alert him to his daughter's dire situation.[60]

In London, in particular, pawnbrokers and marine store dealers were blamed for encouraging servants to commit thefts. In 1816 a witness to the Select Committee on the Police in the Metropolis claimed that there was scarcely 'a chandler's shop in any part of the Metropolis ... but buys old bottles or linen, or any thing that a servant girl... can take with her'. He then added, 'many girls lose their reputation by the encouragement women keeping these shops give them.'[61] It was alleged that some servants even moved rapidly from post to post purely to steal, usually keeping on a room in a lodging-house while they were in a place so that they could return to this and conceal their ill-gotten gains, if they did not pawn them immediately. Some relied on having an accomplice, like Maria Lynch, who stole twelve spoons from her master, a licensed victualler in London, during the mid-1860s. She passed them on to her sister to pawn, without telling the sister apparently that they had

Figure 19. The servant as criminal. Ada Mary Wood, aged 16; imprisoned in Aylesbury gaol for two months with hard labour for stealing a gold locket from her mistress in 1871. (Centre for Buckinghamshire Studies).

been stolen. When the theft was discovered it was found that the sister had divided the spoons and pledged them to three different pawnbrokers. Maria was sentenced to six months' imprisonment at the Old Bailey, but her sister's protestations of innocence concerning the origins of the spoons were accepted by the court and she was found not guilty.[62]

Earlier in the century some relatively minor thefts had attracted far harsher punishments, including the death sentence or transportation to Australia. That could even affect servants who had received gifts from an employer during his or her lifetime but who, after the employer's death, were faced with accusations that the goods had been stolen. One such unfortunate was a Richmond maid, Sarah Wharmby, who on her mistress's death in 1824 was charged by the family with stealing a quilt and other articles. The case was heard at the Surrey Assizes and Sarah was initially sentenced to death, although this was subsequently mitigated to transportation. A campaign was waged by the mistress's friends to have the decision overturned, with all of them attesting to the girl's good character. Their efforts were unsuccessful and a year later when one of them enquired whether the term of transportation could be reduced, he was told that Sarah had sailed 'for Vandiemansland' (modern Tasmania) in September 1824. Nothing had been heard of her since. In the interim her father had died from grief and shame.[63]

False accusations continued to be made in the twentieth century and it was in this context that in July 1920 the Social and Legislation Committee of the Young Women's Christian Association (YWCA) received an appeal from a French maid, who had worked at a house in Berkeley Square, London. She applied to the Association for help in recovering her wages. Her mistress had accused her of stealing silver spoons and had said that only if these were returned would the girl's wages be paid. The maid, in great distress, denied the theft and stated that her mistress drank. She also claimed that she was the only survivor of a staff of servants, the others having been sent away, some also on the pretext that they had stolen goods. The Committee advised the girl to return to her mistress and ask again for her wages, and then leave and go to a hostel of which she knew. She was to report back if the wages were not paid or her trunk was retained. The next day she returned and said that the matter had been satisfactorily settled. Presumably the involvement of the YWCA had had the desired effect.[64] Its records show a number of other cases where its intervention was requested to secure the payment of wages or the recovery of a servant's possessions when these had been retained by an employer on one pretext or another.

Particularly vulnerable to ill-treatment by employers were young workhouse servants who lacked family support. It was the horrific murder of Mary Parsons, a fourteen-year-old orphan from Bideford workhouse by a Devon farmer and his wife in January 1850 that prompted the passage of legislation designed to protect them. Under the 1851 Apprentices and Servants Act the master of any servant or apprentice under the age of eighteen was to supply 'necessary Food, Clothing, or Lodging', something which had not happened in the case of Mary Parsons. Failure to comply could be punished with three years' imprisonment. In addition, where a 'young Person under the Age of Sixteen' was hired out as a servant from a workhouse, he or she was to have at least two visits a year from a poor law official up to the age of sixteen. Such regular contacts might have saved Mary's life. Unfortunately, either through official inertia or because mistresses failed to notify the authorities if a girl moved to a fresh place, this requirement for regular visiting was never fully implemented.[65]

In the early and middle years of the nineteenth century, servants were sometimes prosecuted by their employer if they left their post before their contract of service had expired. Under the Master and Servant Acts they could be punished by up to three months' imprisonment with hard labour. Court and prison records show that a few maids fell victim to this, as in the case of Selina Nutt, aged nineteen, who was a maid at Cokethorpe Park in Oxfordshire. She received a sentence of one month's imprisonment with hard labour for 'leaving her service' in December 1841.[66] Not until 1875 was servant imprisonment as a possible penalty for a breach of the contract of employment finally ended.

Efforts to establish trade unions among servants to improve their pay and conditions of employment, or to provide protection against harsh masters and mistresses, proved unsuccessful in both the nineteenth and twentieth centuries. The diffused nature of domestic service, with workers divided among many different households, and the unwillingness of upper servants and lower servants to co-operate in such activities partly explained this. Employer hostility to trade unionism and the fear of being dismissed without a good character reference also contributed. Servants, too, often lacked the cash to subscribe to union funds, while their long working hours made it difficult to attend meetings.[67]

As regards the broader issue of lawbreaking, overall few domestic workers had brushes with the legal system, either as perpetrators of crime or as victims of malevolent employers. William Lanceley, after a lifetime in service, maintained that dishonesty was 'rare among servants, considering the temptations to which they are exposed and the amount of valuable articles of gold and silver that pass through their hands and which are always within their reach.' In his long career he claimed to have known of only one case of theft, and that was when a silver tankard went missing. It was never found and although a footman was suspected, it could not be traced to him.[68]

Perhaps the last word, though, can be left to an employer, Lady Willoughby de Broke, who wrote in 1916:

> Above all let us not mistrust our servants ... When we think of the amazing trust that perforce we repose in them and how seldom it is abused, we must admit that servants as a class are wonderfully honest. We entrust our jewels and laces to the maid and our valuable plate to the butler with a confidence that is rarely misplaced. Those houses where nothing is kept locked away from the servants are I fancy the most secure of all.[69]

It was a just tribute to what was up to the middle of the twentieth century a major sector of the British labour force. Yet it is one which has for far too long languished in obscurity, 'hidden from history', and neglected by commentators on British social life in past times. Genealogists, by researching their own family background, are helping to remedy this.

A SUMMARY OF SOURCES

Some useful Addresses

COUNTY RECORD OFFICES:
See www.genuki.org.uk for addresses.

THE BODLEIAN LIBRARY,
University of Oxford,
Oxford, OX1 3BG
www.ouls.ox.ac.uk/bodley

THE BRITISH LIBRARY,
St Pancras,
96 Euston Road,
London NW1 2DB
Tel: 0870 444 1500
www.bl.uk

THE BRITISH LIBRARY NEWSPAPER LIBRARY,
Colindale Avenue,
London NW9 5HE
Tel: 020 7412 7353
www.bl.uk/catalogues/newspapers

LONDON METROPOLITAN ARCHIVES,
40 Northampton Road,
London EC1R OHB

Tel: 020 7332 3820
www.cityoflondon.gov.uk/lma

THE NATIONAL ARCHIVES,
Ruskin Avenue, Kew, Richmond, Surrey TW9 4DU
Tel: 020 8876 3440
www.nationalarchives.gov.uk

THE WOMEN'S LIBRARY,
London Metropolitan University,
Old Castle Street,
London E1 7NT
Tel: 020 7320 2222
www.thewomenslibrary.ac.uk

Sources

The location of manuscript and other primary sources consulted is included in the references. The following are general pointers to assist genealogists seeking to trace family members who were in service or wishing to learn something of their daily lives.

(a) **Manuals on Household Management**

There are many of these and the following is just a selection. Examples can be located online through Google Books. The manuals detail servants' duties and sometimes include suggested wage rates. They also advise mistresses on the management of their households.

Samuel and Sarah Adams, *The Complete Servant* (1825). A new, somewhat abbreviated, version of this was published in 1989. It still includes full details of servants' duties.

Mrs. Isabella Beeton, *Book of Household Management* (1861). There have been many editions of this classic work.

Mrs. Florence Caddy, *Household organisation* (1877).

Mrs. Eliza Haweis, *The Art of Housekeeping* (1889)

Mrs. J. E. Panton, *From Kitchen to Garret* (1888) (2nd edn 1893);

The Servants' Practical Guide (1880)

John H. Walsh, *A Manual of Domestic Economy* (1857) (2nd edn 1874)

(b) **Trade Directories**
These are useful for tracing servant registry offices, as are the records of the National Vigilance Association at the Women's Library. The latter records also underline the National Vigilance Association's moral concerns. Servant registry offices advertised in the press, too.

(c) **Newspapers**
Both national and local newspapers include advertisements inserted by, or for, servants, in respect of job vacancies. They often include details of conditions of employment, rates of pay, and special requirements or prohibitions. The trade press, such as *The Gardeners' Chronicle* or, for gamekeepers, *The Field*, *The Shooting Times*, and *The Gamekeeper* list job vacancies and the conditions imposed by employers. They also include obituaries, court cases, and details of successes in competitions, shows, &c. Newspapers in general are an invaluable source of information on working conditions, court cases, and general attitudes towards domestic workers.

(d) **Servants' Wages Books, Household Accounts, Correspondence and Diaries**.
These will usually only survive in the case of larger employers, especially those with landed estates. They give information on the hiring and firing of servants, their pay, and sometimes their working conditions. In a few cases they include details of previous places of employment. These documents may remain with the family but a number can be found in county record offices and archives, local history libraries, and major collections, such as those in the Bodleian Library in Oxford and the British Library in London.

(e) **Census Returns at the National Archives** and elsewhere provide a snapshot of household employment for the years they cover from 1841, and particularly from 1851 to the beginning of the twentieth century. The census records can be searched on line and on microfilm. The census was taken every ten years.

(f) **Poor Law and Charity Records**.
For younger and cheaper servants poor law records in local archives often include details of apprenticeships or of servant recruitment and training arrangements. In the case of London, there are some surviving reports by the Metropolitan Association for Befriending Young Servants on individual maids, in the London Metropolitan Archives.

Charity records frequently include apprenticeship or employment details, as in the case of the Foundling Hospital in London. The Hospital's records are in the London Metropolitan Archives. They include hundreds of petitions from unmarried mothers, many of them servants, seeking to have their child taken into the care of the Hospital. Valuable career profiles of the women and girls concerned are included. Local record offices may have details of charities providing education and training for young servants in their area.

(g) **Training Schemes**

In the nineteenth century, reformatory and industrial schools, poor law institutions and charities all provided training. Details of charitable initiatives in the early 1920s are included in Appendix C of the *Report to the Minister of Labour of the Committee Appointed to Enquire into the Present Conditions as to the Supply of Female Domestic Servants* (HMSO, 1923). In the late 1930s the Young Women's Christian Association provided a training scheme for a small number of Czech refugees and the records of these are at the Modern Records Centre, University of Warwick.

Between the World Wars there were government training schemes set up in areas of high unemployment. Details of these and of individual students attending some of the courses are in the Ministry of Labour records in the National Archives. After 1945 another government initiative led to the setting up of the National Institute of Houseworkers, again to boost the domestic labour force and provide training. The records of this organisation are also in the National Archives, although there is material, too, at the Modern Records Centre, University of Warwick. Lists of those who attended the courses are included in some of the reports.

(h) **Trade Union Records**

These are sparse but the Rule Book and some other material relating to the London and Provincial Domestic Servants' Union (established in 1891) are in the National Archives. Information on the National Domestic Union (formed in 1919), the Domestic Workers' Guild (formed in 1932) and the National Union of Domestic Workers (established in 1938) is available at the Modern Records Centre, University of Warwick. Records relating to the National Union of Domestic Workers are in the National Archives, too.

(i) **Law Breaking**

Court records are preserved in county record offices and, for the Central Criminal Court, at the London Guildhall Library. The transcripts of every trial heard at the Old Bailey from 1674 to 1913 are available free online, along with biographical details of men and women executed at Tyburn (www.oldbaileyonline.org). Court cases also include servants who appeared as witnesses to crimes, as well as perpetrators. Records of Assizes are in the National Archives.

There are prison records in the National Archives and in county record offices, while in the late eighteenth and first half of the nineteenth centuries transportation records to Australia can be linked with trials. These will include servants and are at the National Archives.

Finally, there are consistory court records for the eighteenth and early nineteenth centuries with servants acting as witnesses in cases involving the marital problems of their employers, inheritance disputes, and similar personal matters. For London they are available in the London Metropolitan Archives and for the north of England at the Borthwick Institute of Historical Records, University of York. Records of these church courts survive in some county record offices, for example those for Hampshire and Oxfordshire.

(j) **Probate Records**
Servants, particularly senior ones like housekeepers, butlers, lady's maids, head gardeners and head gamekeepers, may have left Wills, or they may be mentioned in the Will of an employer, especially if they were long-serving and well liked.

(k) **Photographs and Punch Cartoons**
County record offices and local history libraries may have photographs illustrating the dress, the number of servants employed in a household, and sometimes the work performed by domestic and estate workers. In the case of footmen and coachmen, their elaborate liveries indicate their importance as status symbols for their employers. *Punch* cartoons show general attitudes towards servants, often showing them in an unfavourable light, much to the bitter resentment of the workers themselves. Early editions of *Punch* are in major libraries like the Bodleian in Oxford or the British Library but they may exist in larger local libraries as well.

N.B. The British Newspaper Library is scheduled to close in the next year or so. Microfilmed records of newspapers should be available at the British Library in Euston Road. The British Library website will provide up-to-date information.

SUGGESTED READING

John Burnett ed., *Useful Toil. Autobiographies of Working People from the 1820s to the 1920s*, London and New York: Routledge, 1994 edition

William Cresswell, *Diary of a Victorian Gardener. William Cresswell and Audley End*, Swindon: English Heritage, 2006

Frank Dawes, *Not In Front of the Servants. Domestic Service in England 1850-1939*, London: Wayland Publishers, 1973

Jonathan Gathorne-Hardy, *The Rise and Fall of the British Nanny*, London: Hodder and Stoughton, 1972

Jessica Gerard, *Country House Life. Family and Servants 1815-1914*, Oxford: Blackwell, 1994

Mark Girouard, *Life in the English Country House*, London: Book Club Associates, 1979 edition

Rosina Harrison ed., *Gentlemen's Gentlemen*, London: Sphere Books, 1978 edition

Rosina Harrison, *Rose: My Life in Service*, London: Cassell, 1975

J. Jean Hecht, *The Domestic Servant Class in Eighteenth Century England*, London: Routledge & Kegan Paul, 1956

Bridget Hill, *Servants. English Domestics in the Eighteenth Century*, Oxford: Clarendon Press, 1996

Pamela Horn, *Flunkeys and Scullions. Life Below Stairs in Georgian England*, Stroud: Sutton Publishing, 2004

Pamela Horn, *Life Below Stairs in the 20th Century*, Stroud: Sutton Publishing, 2003 edition

Pamela Horn, *The Rise and Fall of the Victorian Servant* Stroud: Sutton Publishing, 2004 edition

Theresa M. McBride *The Domestic Revolution. The Modernisation of Household Service in England and France 1820-1920*, London: Croom Helm, 1976

Tim Meldrum, *Domestic Service and Gender 1660-1750. Life and Work in the London Household*, London: Pearson Education Ltd., 2000

Samuel Mullins and Gareth Griffiths ed., *Cap and Apron. An Oral History of Domestic Service in the Shires, 1880-1950*, Leicestershire Museums, Art Galleries and Records Service: The Harborough Series, No. 2, 1986

Norman Mursell, *Come Dawn, Come Dusk. Fifty Years a Gamekeeper for the Dukes of Westminster*, Cambridge: White Lion Books, 1996 edition

Toby Musgrave, *The Head Gardeners. Forgotten Heroes of Horticulture*, London: Aurum, 2007

Pamela A. Sambrook, *The Country House Servant*, Stroud: Sutton Publishing, 1999

Noel Streatfeild ed., *The Day Before Yesterday. Firsthand Stories of Fifty Years Ago*, London: Collins, 1956

E. S. Turner, *What the Butler Saw. Two Hundred and Fifty Years of the Servant Problem*, London: Michael Joseph, 1962

T. W. Turner, *Memoirs of a Gamekeeper, (Elveden, 1868-1953)*, London: Geoffrey Bles, 1954

Giles Waterfield, Anne French, Matthew Craske, *Below Stairs. 400 Years of Servants' Portraits*, London: National Portrait Gallery, 2004

Merlin Waterson ed., *The Country House Remembered. Recollections of Life Between the Wars*, London and Henley: Routledge & Kegan Paul, 1985

Merlin Waterson, *The Servants' Hall. A Domestic History of Erddig*, London and Henley: Routledge & Kegan Paul, 1980

Margaret Willes, *Country House Estates*, London: The National Trust, 1996

Margaret Willes, *Household Management*, London: The National Trust, 1996

Dorothy Wise ed., *Diary of William Tayler Footman 1837*, London: Westminster City Archives with the St. Marylebone Society, 1998

REFERENCES

N.B. The following abbreviations have been used:
P.P. - Parliamentary Papers
MRC - Modern Records Centre, University of Warwick

Foreword

1 *Report on Post-War Organisation of Private Domestic Employment*, by Violet Markham and Florence Hancock, P.P. 1944-45, Vol. 5, pp.3-5

Chapter 1 Servant Keeping

1. *General Report of the 1881 Census for England and Wales*, P.P. 1883, Vol. 80, p.33.
2. Winifred Foley, *A Child in the Forest,* Coleford: Douglas McLean, 2002 edition, p.146. The book was first published in 1974.
3. A.Hood to the Earl of Rosebery's Secretary, 15 August, 1912 in D/RO/2/73 at the Centre for Buckinghamshire Studies.
4. Eric Horne, *More Winks*, London: T. Werner Laurie, 1932, p.125. Horne had served as a butler for many years.
5. Charles Kightly, *Country Voices. Life and Lore in Farm and Village*, London: Thames & Hudson, 1984, p.155.
6. Memories of Mrs. Florrie Davis (née Stowe), 21 September, 1967 in MS.Top.c.40 at the Bodleian Library, Oxford.
7. Booth MSS. A.29, f.26 at the British Library of Political and Economic Science, London School of Economics.
8. Samuel Mullins and Gareth Griffiths, *Cap and Apron. An Oral History of Domestic Service in the Shires, 1880-1950*, Leicestershire Museums, Art Galleries and Records Service, The Harborough Series, No. 2, 1986, p.28.

9. Foley, *A Child in the Forest*, pp.184-185.

10. Board of Trade (Labour Department): Report by Miss Collet on the Money Wages of Indoor Domestic Servants, London: HMSO C.9346, 1899, p.25.

11. Adeline Hartcup, *Below Stairs in the Great Country Houses*, London: Sidgwick & Jackson, 1980, p.169.

12. Letter from Miss Mildred M. White of Cheltenham to Miss Violet Markham in 1945 in Markham MSS. 12/3 at the British Library of Political and Economic Science, London School of Economics.

Chapter 2 The Daily Round: Indoor Servants

1. J. H. Walsh, *A Manual of Domestic Economy*, London: George Routledge & Sons, 1874 edn., p.224.

2. Details of the hiring of a butler at Englefield House, Berkshire in D/EBy.A.130 at Berkshire Record Office.

3. John Burnett ed., *Useful Toil*, London & New York: Routledge, 1994 edn., pp.223-224.

4. The timetables for the house-parlourmaid and the housemaid in the Sambourne household are at Kensington Local History Library.

5. Leonore Davidoff, *Worlds Between. Historical Perspectives on Gender and Class*, Cambridge: Polity Press, 1995, p.24.

6. Thea Holme, *The Carlyles at Home*, London: Persephone Books, 2002 edn., pp.18 and 165.

7. Pamela Horn, *The Rise and Fall of the Victorian Servant*, Stroud: Sutton Publishing, 2004 edn., pp.131-134 for examples of servant fatalities.

8. Quoted in Geoffrey Tyack, 'Service on the Cliveden Estate Between the Wars' in *Oral History*, Vol. 5, No. 1 (Spring 1977), p.68.

9. Eric Horne, *What the Butler Winked At*, London: T. Werner Laurie Ltd., 1923, p.274.

10. Eileen Kelly ed., *Born to Serve*, Liverpool: Second Chance to Learn, n.d., pp.28-29.

11. Rosina Harrison ed., *Gentlemen's Gentlemen*, London: Sphere Books, 1978 edn., pp.211-213 and 216. Ernest King, *The Green Baize Door*, London: William Kimber, 1963, p.10.

12. Harrison ed., *Gentlemen's Gentlemen*, p.166.

13. Servants' Wages Books for Nuneham Courtenay are at the Bodleian Library, Oxford, MSS.D.D.Harcourt e.45-e.47. Pay Roll No. 1 for Cliveden estate at the Centre for Buckinghamshire Studies in D.158/29.

14. Servants' Wages Books for Nuneham Courtenay MSS.D.D.Harcourt e.45-e.47.

15. William Lanceley, *From Hall-Boy to House-Steward*, London: Edward Arnold & Co., 1925, pp.152-153.

16. Liz Stanley ed., *The Diaries of Hannah Cullwick, Victorian Maidservant*, London: Virago, 1984, pp.152-153.

17. Minnie Cowley, 'Live-in General Maid' in *Spare Rib*, March 1976, No. 44, p.36.

18. Ethel M. Sims from Kensal Rise, London to Violet Markham in 1945 in Markham MSS. 12/6. Mrs. Sims was a war widow.

19. Englefield House Servants' Book, D/EBy.A.130 at Berkshire Record Office.

20. Housekeeper's Book for Nuneham Courtenay, MSS.D.D.Harcourt e.44 at the Bodleian Library, Oxford.

21. Pamela A. Sambrook, *The Country House Servant*, Stroud: Sutton Publishing, 1999, p.99.

22. See correspondence in the Carnarvon MSS at Hampshire Record Office, 75M91/L31/9 and 75M91/L31/8.

23. Notes concerning applicants for the post of lady's maid: comment on Emma Brown, aged 32 and the daughter of a gardener. In MSS.D.D.Harcourt e.19, f.10.

24. Rosina Harrison, *Rose: My Life in Service*, London: Cassell, 1975, pp.32 and 64.

25. Mary Anne Disraeli: Household Accounts 1845-49, MS.Dep.Hughenden 314/1 at the Bodleian Library.

26. Merlin Waterson ed., *The Country House Remembered. Recollections of Life Between the Wars*, London: Routledge & Kegan Paul, 1985, p.180.

27. Horn, *Rise and Fall of the Victorian Servant*, p.67.

28. Alice Slater to Charles C. Edmunds, 13 December, 1912 in Rosebery MSS. D/RO/2/73 at the Centre for Buckinghamshire Studies. See also her letter of 20 January, 1913, when she noted she had supplied 'meals to a huge number more this last December than were supplied in the December previous', and that Lord Rosebery himself had decided where 'the Turtle Soup shall be ordered from'.

29. *Buckinghamshire Within Living Memory*, Buckinghamshire Federation of Women's Institutes: Newbury: Countryside Books, 1993, p.144.

30. Sambrook, *The Country House Servant*, p.78.

31. King, *The Green Baize Door*, p.21.

32. Sambourne diaries at Kensington Local History Library, entries for 2 May, 1883 and 13 August, 1886 for example.

33. Pamela Watkin ed., *A Kingston Lacy Childhood. Reminiscences of Viola Bankes*, Wimborne: The Dovecote Press Ltd., 1989 edn., pp.19-22.

34. Noel Streatfeild ed., *The Day 'Before Yesterday*, London: Collins, 1956, p.17.

35. Barbara Charlton, *Recollections of a Northumbrian Lady 1815-1866*, Stocksfield: The Spredden Press, 1989 edn., p.195.

36. Charles Edmunds to Lord Rosebery, 21 October, 1911 in D/RO/2/67 at the Centre for Buckinghamshire Studies.

37. Mrs. Isabella Beeton, *Book of Household Management*, London: Ward Lock & Co., 1899 edn.), p.1462.

38. Servants' Wages Book for Nuneham Courtenay MSS.D.D.Harcourt e.47, for the period 1878-85.

39. Dorothy Wise ed., *Diary of William Tayler Footman 1837*, London: Westminster City Archives with the St. Marylebone Society, 1998, pp. 31 and 38.

40. Petworth. *The Servants' Quarters*, London: The National Trust, 1997, p.4.

41. Quoted in Horn, *Rise and Fall of the Victorian Servant*, p.88.

42. Waterson ed., *The Country House Remembered*, p.177.

43. Watkin ed., *A Kingston Lacy Childhood*, pp.. 64-68.

44. Harrison ed., *Gentlemen's Gentlemen*, pp.146-147.

45. King, *The Green Baize Door*, pp.12-13.

46. Eric Horne, *What the Butler Winked At*, London: T. Werner Laurie Ltd.' 1923, pp.76-77.

47. E. S. Turner, *What the Butler Saw. Two hundred and fifty years of the servant problem*, London: Michael Joseph, 1962, p.170.

48. Mary Anne Disraeli: Household Accounts 1~45-49, MS.Dep.Hughenden 314/1.

49. Sambrook, *The Country House Servant*, p.29.

50. Petworth. *The Servants' Quarters*, p.18.

51. Lord Rosebery's Instructions to his Agent, Charles C. Edmunds: Memorandum for Instruction, 14 February, 1912 in D/RO/2/67. Cook's Journal for 1911 in D/RO/1/67 and Cook's Ledger D/RO/1/65 for 1911. Letter from E. Chevalier to Charles C. Edmunds, 9 August, 1912, in D/RO/2/73 at the Centre for Buckinghamshire Studies.

52. Quoted in Horn, *Rise and Fall of the Victorian Servant*, p.95.

53. Quoted in Turner, *What the Butler Saw*, p.158.

Chapter 3 The Daily Round: Outdoor Workers

1. Merlin Waterson, *The Servants' Hall. A Domestic History of Erddig*, London and Henley: Routledge & Kegan Paul, 1980, p.69.

2. Tyack, 'Service on the Cliveden Estate Between the Wars', p.66. Gervas Huxley, Victorian Duke. The Life of Hugh Lupus Grosvenor First Duke of Westminster (London: Oxford University Press, 1967), pp. 137-138.

3. Arthur Richard Inch, *Reminiscences of a Life in Private Service*, London: Trinity Press, n.d. [c.1998], pp.19-21.

4. Waterson ed., *The Country House Remembered*, p.178.

5. Margaret Willes, *Country House Estates*, London: National Trust, 1996, p.4.

6. Petworth. *The Servants' Quarters*, p.2.

7. *General Report of the 1911 Census of Population for England and Wales*, P.P. 1913, Vol. 78, p.xxviii.

8. Kedrun Laurie, *Cricketer Preferred. Estate Workers at Lyme Park 1898-1946*, Lyme Park Joint Committee, 1979, p.21.

9. Basil and Jessie Harley ed., *A Gardener at Chatsworth. Three Years in the Life of Robert Aughtie 1848-1850*, Hanley Swan: The Self Publishing Association, 1992, p.20.

10. Kate Colquhoun *'The Busiest Man in England': A Life of Joseph Paxton*, Boston: David R. Godine, 2006 edn., pp. 36 and 152. Willes, Country House Estates, p.18.

11. Richard Greville Verney Lord Willoughby de Broke, *The Passing Years*, London: Constable & Company Ltd., 1924, p.49.

12. Howard Colvin, *Calke Abbey, Derbyshire. A Hidden House Revealed*, London: Antler Books edn., 1985, pp. 71 and 73.

13. Bob Gregory, *A Gardener's Life. Memories of Gardening on some of the great English private estates*, Privately printed, n.d. [c. 1999], pp.56-58.
14. *The Gardeners' Chronicle*, 8 January, 1876.
15. Jane Brown, *The Pursuit of Paradise. A Social History of Gardens and Gardening*, London: Harper Collins, 2000 edn., p.257.
16. Laurie, *Cricketer Preferred*, pp.22-23.
17. Toby Musgrave, *The Head Gardener: Forgotten Heroes of Horticulture*, London: Aurum Press Ltd., 2007, p.77.
18. Bulstrode Park MSS. D/RA/5/60 at the Centre for Buckinghamshire Studies.
19. Harley ed., *A Gardener at Chatsworth*, p.114.
20. William Cresswell, *Diary of a Victorian Gardener. William Cresswell and Audley End*, Swindon: English Heritage, 2006, pp.20-21 and 23.
21. Harley ed., *A Gardener at Chatsworth*, p.185.
22. Colquhoun, *'The Busiest Man in England'*, p.31.
23. Gregory, *A Gardener's Life*, p.6.
24. Brown, *The Pursuit of Paradise*, p.256.
25. Tyack, *'Service on the Cliveden Estate'*, pp.75-76.
26. *The Gardeners' Chronicle*, 19 June, 1875.
27. Brown, *The Pursuit of Paradise*, p.260. Waterson ed., *The Country House Remembered*, p.152.
28. Regina Marler ed., *Selected Letters of Vanessa Bell*, London: Bloomsbury, 1993, p.468.
29. J. Jean Hecht, *The Domestic Servant Class in Eighteenth-Century England*, London: Routledge & Kegan Paul, 1956, p.120.
30. Mary Anne Disraeli's Household Accounts, Dep.Hughenden 314/1, entry for 26 June, 1849, in the Bodleian Library.
31. Turner, *What the Butler Saw*, p.176.
32. Beeton, *Book of Household Management*, 1861 edn., pp.976-977.
33. The Marchioness of Bath, *Before the Sunset Fades*, Longleat: The Longleat Estate Company, 1967 edn., pp.12-13.
34. Kightly, *Country Voices*, pp.163-165.
35. Michael Astor, *Tribal Feeling*, London: John Murray, 1963, p.65.
36. Tyack, *'Service on the Cliveden Estate'*, p.73.
37. Nuneham Courtenay Wages Books, MS.D.D.Harcourt e.45; MS.D.D.Harcourt e.46; and MS.D.D.Harcourt e.3 at the Bodleian Library.
38. Paula Snyder ed., *Great Estates*, London: Channel 4 Television, 2000, p.14
39. Jeri Bapasola, *Household Matters. Domestic Service at Blenheim Palace*, Woodstock: Blenheim Palace, 2007, p.55.
40. Tyack, *'Service on the Cliveden Estate'*, p.73.
41. T. W. Turner, *Memoirs of a Gamekeeper. Elveden 1868-1953*, London: Geoffrey Bles, 1954, p.142, Appendix A. J. Mordaunt Crook, *The Rise of the Nouveaux Riches*, London: John Murray, 2000 edn., pp.268-269.

42. Jonathan Ruffer, *The Big Shots. Edwardian Shooting Parties*, London: Quiller Press, 1997 edn., p.126.

43. Pamela Horn, *Flunkeys and Scullions*, Stroud: Sutton Publishing, 2004, p. 184.

44. *General Report of the Census of Population for England and Wales 1901*, London: HMSO, 1904 and *General Report of the Census of Population for England and Wales*, 1911, P.P.1913, Vol. 78.

45. Steve Humphries and Beverley Hopwood ed., *Green and Pleasant Land. The Untold Story of Country Life in Twentieth Century* Britain, London: Channel 4 Books, 1999, p.73.

46. Turner, *Memoirs of a Gamekeeper*, p.115.

47. *The Gamekeeper*, February 1900.

48. Norman Mursell, *Come Dawn, Come Dusk. Fifty Years a Gamekeeper for the Dukes of Westminster*, Cambridge: White Lion Books, 1996 edn., pp. 3 and 9.

49. Ruffer, *The Big Shots*, pp.127-130.

50. Turner, *Memoirs of a Gamekeeper*, p.42.

51. *Report of the Select Committee on the Game Laws*, P.P.1873, Vol. 13, Qu.3028, evidence of Thomas Purves, a tenant farmer from Caithness.

52. *Report of the Select Committee on the Game Laws*, P.P.1872, Vol. 10, Qu.1616-1617, evidence of Fairman Joseph Mann, tenant of Church Farm, Shropham, Norfolk, since 1862.

53. Humphries and Hopwood ed., *Green and Pleasant Land*, p.47.

54. Turner, *Memoirs of a Gamekeeper*, p.94.

55. *The Gamekeeper*, January 1900.

56. *The Shooting Times*, 7 January, 1893.

57. Englefield House Servants' Book D/EBy A.130 at Berkshire Record Office, entry for Lady Day, 1885.

58. Game Book for Nuneham Park, MSS.D.D.Harcourt c.558 and Account of Game Consumed at Nuneham Courtenay, MSS.D.D.Harcourt e.49 at the Bodleian Library.

59. Game Book for the Mentmore Estate, D/RO/l/60 at the Centre for Buckinghamshire Studies.

60. Brian P. Martin, *Tales of the Old Gamekeepers*, Newton Abbot: David & Charles, 1999 edn., p.11. Pamela Horn, *Life Below Stairs in the 20th Century*, Stroud: Sutton Publishing, 2003 edn., pp.136-139.

Chapter 4 Hiring, Firing and Moving On

1. See *General Report of the 1911 Census of Population for England and Wales*, p.xxvi.

2. Burnett ed., *Useful Toil*, p.131.

3. Charles Booth, *Life and Labour of the People in London. Second Series: Industry, Vol. 8*, London: Macmillan, 1903, p.214.

4. Diaries of Marion Sambourne at Kensington Local History Library, entry for 18 February, 1885. The entry was written in French, perhaps to defeat prying servant eyes.

5. Norman S. B. Gras and Ethel C. Gras, *The Economic and Social History of an English Village*, Cambridge, Mass.: Harvard University Press, 1930, p.157.

6. Beeton, *Book of Household Management*, 1861, p.7.
7. Diaries of Marion Sambourne, entries for 24 January, 1883 and 30 January, 1885.
8. Mullins and Griffiths ed., *Cap and Apron*, pp. 8-9 and 12.
9. Frederick John Gorst, *Of Carriages and Kings*, London: W. H. Allen, 1956, pp.120-122.
10. Holme, *The Carlyles at Home*, pp.186-187.
11. Anne Sturges-Bourne to Marianne Dyson, 13 August, 1850, 9M55/F25/15 at Hampshire Record Office. The other correspondence between Anne Sturges-Bourne and Marianne Dyson is also at Hampshire Record Office.
12. Mothers' Petitions Accepted, in the Foundling Hospital archives A/FH/A8/1/2/65/1-, application made on 22 July, 1856, at the London Metropolitan Archives. In January 1855 Nancy had got to know Thomas Folley, an engineer, and in February 1856 she gave birth to his child. She last saw him in June 1855.
13. King, *The Green Baize Door*, p.19.
14. Humphries and Hopwood ed., *Green and Pleasant Land*, pp.28-29.
15. Helme, *The Carlyles at Home*, pp.163 and 188-189.
16. Horn, *Life Below Stairs in the 20th Century*, p.6.
17. *The Lady*, 20 February, 1890.
18. Horn, *The Rise and Fall of the Victorian Servant*, p.33.
19. *Domestic Help*, 3 January and 24 January, 1885, advertisement for Auckland Servants' Registry, New Zealand, T. B. Hannaford, Proprietor.
20. Frank Dawes, *Not in Front of the Servants. Domestic Service in England 1850-1939*, London: Wayland Publishers, 1973, p.103.
21. Theresa M. McBride, *The Domestic Revolution. The Modernization of Household Service in England and France 1820-1920*, New York: Holmes & Meier edn., 1976, p.77.
22. *Domestic News*, April 1915 and December 1917, at the British Library, P.P.1103.abf.
23. Masters' comments at Easter 1853, A/FH/A12/10/100 at the London Metropolitan Archives, which holds all the Foundling Hospital documents referred to.
24. A Foundling, '*The Child She Bare*', (London: Headley Bros. Publishers Ltd., n.d. [1919]), pp. 124, 126, 129 and 169. For details of Hannah Sherman see Register of Apprentices A/FH/A12/3/3 and Masters' comments, Whitsun 1884, A/FH/ A12/10/131.
25. For Matilda Burney see Register of Apprentices, A/FH/A12/3/3; Secretary's letter book 1853-1857, A/FH/A/6/2/12, ff. 48, 197, 361 and 442-443; Masters' comments on Apprentices Easter 1854, A/FH/A12/10/101 and Easter 1856, A/FH/A12/10/103. Meeting of the General Committee/on Film 0041/31, meeting on 11 April, 1857.
26. Kensington Union Schools (Banstead): Report of Girls under the Care of the Metropolitan Association for Befriending Young Servants, 1907, KBG.211, at the London Metropolitan Archives.
27. Central London School District Records of Service Girls, CLSD/246, for example, for the early 1930s, at the London Metropolitan Archives.

28. Bicester Poor Law Union Minute Book for 1875/76, PLU2/G/1Al/21, entries for 6 August, 1875 and 14 and 21 January, 1876 and PLU2/G/1Al/22, entry for 15 December, 1876, at Oxfordshire Record Office.

29. *Third Annual Report of the Local Government Board*: 'Report by Mrs. Nassau Senior as to the effect on Girls of the system of education at Pauper Schools', P.P.1874, Vol. 25, p.355, case no. 4.

30. Walter Monnington, *Our London Poor Law Schools*, London: Eyre & Spottiswoode, 1898, pp. 5 and 182.

31. Joan Rimmer, *Yesterday's Naughty Children. Training Ship, Girls' Reformatory and Farm School. A History of the Liverpool Reformatory Association, founded in 1855*, Manchester: Neil Richardson, 1986, pp.52-54.

32. Charles W. Cooper, *Town and County or Forty Years in Private Service with the Aristocracy*, London: Lovat Dickson, 1937, p.47.

33. James T. Covert, *A Victorian Family as seen Through the Letters of Louise Creighton to her Mother*, Lampeter: The Edwin Mellen Press Ltd., 1998, p.109. This letter was written on 30 January 1876.

34. Waterson ed., *The Country House Remembered*, p.184.

35. See Mary Anne Disraeli's Household Books at the Bodleian Library, MSS.Dep.Hughenden 314/1-3.

36. Letter sent to the author in 1974 by a descendant of the maid.

37. See the servants' book of Mrs. Sally Davis of Bloxham, Oxfordshire in Pamela Horn, 'A Bloxham Servants' Book' in *Cake and Cockhorse*, Spring 2001, Vol. 15, No. 2, p.70. These were excuses made by cooks who left in a few weeks.

38. Beeton, *Book of Household Management*, (1861), pp.6-7.

39. *Annual Report of the Girls' Friendly Society for 1890*, pp.10-11. At that date it estimated its domestic servant members to number 'not less than 80,000'.

40. Horn, *The Rise and Fall of the Victorian Servant*, p.47.

41. London County Council: Employment Agencies: Miscellaneous Printed Reports, PC/EMP/3/1, by-law No. 9 at the London Metropolitan Archives.

42. *Report of the Public Control Committee* in PC/EMP/3/1, 19 February and 5 March, 1909, pp. 1 and 2.

43. *Ministry of Labour: Report to the Minister of Labour of the Committee Appointed to Enquire into the Present Conditions as to the Supply of Female Domestic Servants*, HMSO, 1923, pp.21-23.

44. F.A.R. Sempkins, 'Daughters of Despair' in *Tit-Bits*, 2 March, 1935, p.3.

45. National Vigilance Association archives at the Women's Library, London. Employment Agencies NVA/07/04, Box FL.100, concerning Mrs. Nicholls' Agency, South Shields and Ivy Dawson.

46. National Vigilance Association archives: Employment Agencies, concerning Mrs. Nicholls and the Clayton Agency, Sunderland; Mr. and Mrs. Blackman and Ada Wilkinson, February 1934.

47. National Vigilance Association archives: Employment Agencies, Kensington Domestic Agency of Kilburn, London and Newcastle-on-Tyne, Mrs. Colman of Stamford Hill and Annie Lishman, aged 21, interview on 22 March, 1934.

48. London County Council: Employment Agencies: Complaints Register, PC/EMP/l/7 at the London Metropolitan Archives, cases no. 23 and 35.

49. Quoted in Horn, *Below Stairs in the 20th Century*, p.57.

50. *Annual Reports of the Ministry of Labour for 1927 and 1936*, P.P.1928, Vol. 11 and P.P.1936-37, Vol. 12, p.14, respectively.

51. *Second Report of the Royal Commission on the Employment of Children, Young Persons and Women in Agriculture*, P.P.1868-69, Vol. 13, Minutes of Evidence, pp.355-356.

52. Pamela Horn, 'Ministry of Labour female training programmes between the wars: 1919-39' in *History of Education*, Vol. 31, No. 1, 2002, p.72.

53. Horn, 'Ministry of Labour female training programmes', p.77 and Pamela Horn, 'Hunting the servants. The role of servant training centres between the wars' in *Genealogists' Magazine*, December 1999, p.297.

54. Horn, *Ministry of Labour female training programmes*, p.81.

55. Central Committee on Women's Training and Employment: Centre at Tonypandy (Ystrad) in the Rhondda for Women and Girls in LAB.2/1365/ED730/19/1929 at the National Archives.

56. Central Committee on Women's Training and Employment: Centre for Training in Homecraft and Allied Subjects, Stanhope House, South Shields, LAB.2/1365/ET5707/1933/PT1, at the National Archives.

57. See correspondence with and about Doris Clarke in connection with the South Shields Centre in LAB.2/1365/ED730/18/1929 at the National Archives.

58. Horn, *Hunting the servants*, p.58.

59. Mullins and Griffiths, *Cap and Apron*, p.30.

60. Mullins and Griffiths, *Cap and Apron*, p.30.

61. Horn, *Life Below Stairs in the 20th Century*, pp.244-245.

62. Horn, *Life Below Stairs in the 20th Century*, p.256.

63. National Institute of Housecraft (a change of name from Houseworkers): Correspondence with the Department of Employment, 1971, meeting on 13 January, 1971, in LAB.70/10 at the National Archives. Copies of *The Houseworker* are also in the National Archives and at the MRC, University of Warwick.

64. Horn, *Life Below Stairs in the 20th Century*, p.262.

65. Mullins and Griffiths, *Cap and Apron*, p.37. Horn, *Life Below Stairs in the 20th Century*, p.249.

Chapter 5 Social Relationships

1. *Unemployment Assistance Board Memorandum No. 311. Resident Domestic Servants employed in Private Domestic Service*, in Markham MSS. 6/14, No. 311, at the British Library for Social and Political Science, London School of Economics.

2. C. V. Butler, *Domestic Service. An Enquiry by the Women's Industrial Council*, London: G. Bell & Sons Ltd., 1916, p.14.

3. Butler, *Domestic Service*, p.13.

4. *Report of the Work and Progress of the Girls' Friendly Society in 1887*, London: Hatchards, 1888, pp.11-12.

5. *Domestic News*, April, July and September, 1915.

6. Quoted in Mullins and Griffiths, *Cap and Apron*, p.13.

7. Howard and Peter Coombs ed., *Journal of a Somerset Rector 1803-1834. John Skinner*, Oxford: Oxford University Press, 1984 edn., p.174.

8. John R. Gillis, 'Servants, Sexual Relations and the Risks of Illegitimacy' in *Sex and Class in Women's History*, ed., Judith L. Newton, Mary P. Ryan and Judith R. Walkowitz, London: Boston, Melbourne and Henley: Routledge & Kegan Paul, 1983, pp. 122 and 144.

9. Mullins and Griffiths, *Cap and Apron*, p.16.

10. Butler, *Domestic Service*, p.37.

11. *Ministry of Labour. Report ... as to the Supply of Female Domestic Servants*, 1923, p.16.

12. Jessica Gerard, *Country House Life. Family and Servants, 1815-1914*, (Oxford: Blackwell, 1994), p.235.

13. Mrs. E. Timms of Chadlington, Oxfordshire to the author, 10 September, 1974.

14. Wise ed., *Diary of William Tayler*, p.42.

15. Tyack, *Service on the Cliveden Estate*, p.81.

16. Margaret Llewelyn Davies, *Life As We Have Known It*, London: Virago, 1977 edn., pp.22-29.

17. Nina Slingsby-Smith, *George, Memoirs of a Gentleman's Gentleman*, London: Century, 1986 edn., p.26.

18. Lanceley, *From Hall-Boy to House-Steward*, p.23.

19. Hose Gibbs, *In Service. Rose Gibbs Remembers*, Archives for Brassingbourn & Comberton Village Colleges, 1981, pp.14-15.

20. Inch, *Reminiscences of a Life in Private Service*, p.65.

21. *Ministry of Reconstruction: Report on Domestic Service*, P.P.1919, Vol. 29, p.27.

22. Horn, *Life Below Stairs in the 20th Century*, p.260.

23. Mullins and Griffiths, *Cap and Apron*, p.31.

24. *Report of the Work and Progress of the Girls' Friendly Society in 1889*, London: Rivington, 1890), pp.104-105.

25. Dawes, *Not in Front of the Servants*, p.126.

26. Diary of Grace Germany at the British Library, ADD.MSS.83203, for 5 March, 1922 and ADD.MSS.83204, for 6 October, 1924.

27. Mollie Hardwick, *Mrs. Dizzy, the Life of Mary Anne Disraeli,Viscountess Beaconsfield*, London: Cassell, 1972, p.141

28. Household Book of Mary Anne Disraeli MSS Hughenden 314/4, entry for 19 May, 1857.

29. Mary Anne Disraeli's Household Accounts, MSS.Dep.Hughenden 314/3-4, entries for 20 and 25 April, 1855. W. G. Wiebe, Mary S. Millar, and Ann P. Robson ed., *Benjamin Disraeli Letters*, Vol. 6, 1852-1856, Toronto: University of Toronto Press, 1997, p.493, no. 2855.

30. Horne, *More Winks*, p.58.

31. Sambrook, *The Country House Servant*, pp. 57 and 62.

32. Sambrook, *The Country House Servant*, p.59. Kitty Fisher, 'Life Below Stairs' in *Staffordshire History*, Vol. 3 (Autumn 1985), p.13.

33. Marchioness of Bath, *Before the Sunset Fades*, pp. 17-18.

34. Marchioness of Bath, *Before the Sunset Fades*, p.20.

35. Sambrook, *The Country House Servant*, pp. 57-58.

36. Mark Girouard ed., *A Country House Companion*, London: Century, 1987, p.139.

37. Mullins and Griffiths, *Cap and Apron*, p.13.

38. Lanceley, *From Hall-Boy to House-Steward*, p.161.

39. James Drummond, *Upstairs to Downstairs. Advice to Servant Girls and Weary Mothers*, Aberdeen: Aberdeen University Press, 1991 edn., pp. 3 and 7-10.

40. Drummond, *Upstairs to Downstairs*, p.3.

41. Mary Anne Disraeli's Household Accounts, MSS.Dep.Hughenden 314/3-4, entry for 20 November, 1855, for example. A further 2s. 6d. was given to the coachman.

42. Fisher, *Life Below Stairs*, p.13.

43. Harrison, *Rose: My Life in Service*, p.15.

44. Cooper, *Town and County*, pp.96-98 and 144-145.

45. *Annual Report of Queen Charlotte's Lying-In Hospital, 1884*, H.27/QC/A/027/018, p.24, at the London Metropolitan Archives. Other records, such as Hospital admission books are also at the London Metropolitan Archives. Gillis, 'Servants, Sexual Relations and the Risks of Illegitimacy', pp.138 and 144.

46. Gillis, 'Servants, Sexual Relations and the Risks of Illegitimacy', p.138.

47. Foundling Hospital: Mothers' Petitions for 1875, A/FH/A8/1/2/84/1-, case of Anna Maria Darvill.

48. Foundling Hospital: Mothers' Petitions for 1875, A/FH/A8/1/2/84/1-, case of Alice Tamplin. Several letters from Middlemiss (which he signed 'Old Wagg') to Alice, whom he addressed as 'Dear Dol', survive in the archives. In one he declared: 'Love & kisses to you & baby... Every day I am going after places & I hope I shall soon get one for I have nearly got one & a good one'.

49. Foundling Hospital: Mothers' Petitions for 1859, A/FH/A8/1/2/68/1-, case of Elizabeth Finck. Pamela Horn, 'Victorian Servants' Lives and Mothers' Petitions for the London Foundling Hospital' in *Genealogists' Magazine*, Vol. 29, No. 8 (December 2008), pp.295-296.

50. Ann R. Higginbotham, '"Sin of the Age": Infanticide and Illegitimacy in Victorian London' in *Victorian Scandals. Representations of Gender and Class*, Kristine Ottesen Garrigan ed., Athens, USA: Ohio University Press, 1992, p.267.

51. *Report of the Capital Punishment Commission*, P.P.1866, Vol. 21, evidence of the Revd. Lord Sydney Godolphin Osborne, p.424, Qu.3299.

52. Higginbotham, '"Sin of the Age" ', pp. 265, 269 and 274.

53. Aylesbury Gaol Records: Chaplain's Prisoners' Character Book 1853-54, Q/AG/27, No. 651 at the Centre for Buckinghamshire Studies.

54. Higginbotham, ' "Sin of the Age"', p.262.

55. Streatfeild ed., *The Day Before Yesterday*, p.87.

56. Charlton, *Recollections of a Northumbrian Lady*, p.278.

57. Hartcup, *Below Stairs in the Great Country Houses*, p.192.

58. Hartcup, *Below Stairs in the Great Country Houses*, p.192.

59. Aylesbury Gaol Receiving Book 1870-71, Q/AG/23, No. 4322 and Aylesbury Gaol: Chaplain's Prisoners' Character Book 1871, (Q/AG/29, No. 4322, both at the Centre for Buckinghamshire Studies.

60. Aylesbury Gaol: Chaplain's Prisoners' Character Book 1853-54, Q/AG/27, No. 912.

61. Quoted in Horn, *Flunkeys and Scullions*, p.259.

62. Central Criminal Court Sessions Papers, 11 January, 1865, pp.220-221.

63. V. A. C. Gatrell, *The Hanging Tree. Execution and the English People 1770-1868*, Oxford: Oxford University Press, 1996 edn., pp.428-429.

64. The Archives of the Young Women's Christian Association: Social and Legislation Committee Minutes, MSS.243/139/1, entry for 15 July, 1920, at MRC, University of Warwick. See also entry for 27 October, 1921, when a children's nurse had been dismissed with a month's wages less 10s. She asked for advice about recovering the missing 10s.

65. Horn, *The Rise and Fall of the Victorian Servant*, pp.131-133.

66. Oxford Prison Nominal Register, 1840-1844 at Oxfordshire Record Office, entry for 21 December, 1841. See also case of Elizabeth Walton, aged twenty, also sentenced to one month's hard labour, 1 November, 1842, for 'Leaving her Service'. .

67. Horn, *The Rise and Fall of the Victorian Servant*, pp.173-175 and 202-203. Horn, *Life Below Stairs in the 20th Century*, pp.184-191.

68. Lanceley, *From Hall-Boy to House-Steward*, pp.161-163.

69. Butler, *Domestic Service*, p.108.

INDEX

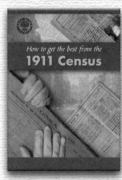
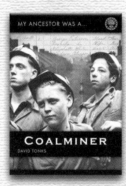